# *Voluntary Islam*

## Davi Barker

*Dedicated in loving memory to my dear friend and spiritual teacher Khadija Jamal Chishty (1936-2011) who taught me that when the giants in your life pass away it's time to stop being small.*

# Voluntary Islam

## Davi Barker

FREE PRESS PUBLICATIONS

Published by Free Press Publications
http://FPP.cc

ISBN: 978-1-938357-02-2

FREE PRESS PUBLICATIONS

Free Press Publications is an independent alternative media and publishig company, founded in June 2009, with the mission of "ensuring a FREE PRESS for the FREEDOM MOVEMENT" and is committed to spreading the message of peace, freedom, love and liberty.

# Introduction

## My Political Agnosticism

In elementary school, I was instructed to recite the Pledge of Allegiance. I refused, insisting that I could not make a pledge until I understood what it meant. I was sent to the principal's office and ordered to do as I was told. For a while I stood with the class, but didn't speak the words, until I was caught. Then I stood and spoke the words, but didn't place my hand over my heart. Again I was caught. It was not until I was sufficiently bullied and humiliated by the teacher that I finally complied. The meaning was never explained to me.

In 2003 I decided to take a semester off school to beg for change along Pacific Avenue in Santa Cruz, California. I didn't need the money, I just wanted the experience. So, I took everything I earned each day and gave it to the other panhandlers around me, since they likely would have received it if I hadn't been there. My favorite strategy was to sit in a meditative position with one palm extended and the other holding a sign that read "TAKE OR GIVE." Some people would drop coins. Others would take coins. One day a police officer approached me and told me that panhandling was illegal. I calmly informed him that I was not panhandling—that the coins in my hand and on the ground were not mine, but had been left there by other people for someone else to take, and he was free to take them. He then informed me that sitting on the sidewalk was illegal and ordered me to move. I respectfully asked him if he would enforce such an ordinance on a statue of Buddha that was sitting nearby with coins in its hand. He said no. So, I graciously requested that I be given the same religious freedom as the statue, to emulate the prophetic practice of sitting still and keeping quiet. He said he had better things to do than argue the Constitution with me. I thanked him, and invited him to tend to those things. Befuddled, he left me alone, and I spent the day thinking about money.

The struggle I'd adopted was to attempt to have no concern whether a person took a coin or gave one, and to feel no attachment to the coins that people gave, realizing that the next person could just as easily take them. In a flash it came to me that the money is nothing at all. Just an intermediate step between goods and services. It cannot be eaten like grain. It cannot be used in manufacturing like petroleum. It is not backed by gold or silver. There is no material difference between notes which at that time I erroneously thought were printed by the Treasury, and notes printed by some cartel of counterfeiters. It is some kind of magic, and the public's pathological belief in that magic. In short, the dollar is backed by faith, and in reality it has little more in common with the value it represents than the statue has in common with the prophet it represents. They are intermediaries.

I began spending hours scouring through the Congressional Record trying to make sense of this strange machine. It was in those volumes that I discovered an unlikely ally in Texas Republican Dr. Ron Paul. In 2007 I joined the Ron Paul Revolution. Contrary to the common narrative, the Tea Party began during the Bush Administration, not in response to Obama. It was not an angry mob of right-wing extremists eager to purge American society of Muslims and Mexicans—it began as a broad coalition of thousands of people from the right and left, brought together under a common banner, by their mutual disgust with the two-man con of party politics, to put an end to war, and abolish the Federal Reserve.

That year, on the anniversary of the Boston Tea Party, major demonstrations took place in every major city in the country. In San Francisco hundreds of us occupied the Federal Reserve building and marched to the bay carrying tea crates labeled with all the government predations we abhorred. Then we chucked them off a pier. (All tethered, of course. San Franciscans are nothing if not environmentally conscious.)

A revolutionary spirit had seized us. It was as if we were confronting the most implacable of enemies, armed only with virtue. We had seen the face of the Leviathan and said, "Not one step farther! You have trampled on mankind long enough." It really seemed that the tide of authoritarianism had reached its high mark and would finally begin to recede. For a brief moment the future seemed bright. I had found a political home among the libertarians.

The descent of the Tea Party reminds me in many ways of Malcolm X's description of the 1963 March on Washington. In his autobiography he explained that the idea began as something "spontaneous, unorganized, and leaderless." But moneyed interests quickly made massive donations to the "big six" civil rights leaders most amicable to Washington DC, who promptly infiltrated the movement, co-opted the planning of the march, and transformed it into "a circus" so tightly controlled that participants were told what signs to carry, what songs to sing, what speeches they could and couldn't make, and ultimately that they had to leave by sunset. Like the 1963 March on Washington, the Tea Party was an authentic expression of public outrage hijacked by the same entrenched powers it aimed to disrupt.

When Dr. Paul lost the nomination, I considered casting my vote for Barack Obama because I had been conditioned, like most

Americans, to believe that voting for the lesser of two evils is preferable to not voting at all. But during the campaign Senator Obama said something to the Military Times that sent me on a political odyssey the end of which I have not yet reached. "What essentially sets a nation-state apart," he told them, "is a monopoly on violence."

This was no political gaffe. The phrase originates from Max Weber's definition of government: "a human community that (successfully) claims the monopoly of the legitimate use of physical force within a given territory." Weber's definition is widely accepted by most political scientists, and he is regarded as the principal thinker in Western statecraft.

I know they tell us that honor belongs to Thomas Jefferson, but don't kid yourself. Weber was one of the architects of the Constitution of the Weimar Republic, specifically Article 48, which empowered the president to unilaterally suspend all the civil rights guaranteed by other articles in the name of national security. That included privacy in the home, privacy in correspondence, freedom of expression, freedom of assembly, the right to form religious societies, and the right to own private property. Article 48 gave Adolf Hitler the legal authority to suppress opposition and obtain dictatorial powers. Indeed, when one claims a monopoly on violence, the pretense of liberty is merely a platitude.

The political climate in America today owes more to Max Weber than any of its own founders, and the powers usurped by its Presidents have more similitude with Article 48 of the Constitution of the Weimar Republic than any article in the US Constitution. Learning this, and understanding it deep in my bones, has changed the way I think about politics forever.

Gandhi told his grandson, "Be the change you want to see in the world." Muslims might express the same idea as "Your means must contain your ends." Fundamentally, the means of violence can never achieve their opposite. So, if we know that a monopoly is economically undesirable, and that violence is morally undesirable, why is a violent monopoly desirable at all?

Many people call me an anarchist for even asking that. Yet it was the question foremost in my mind when I began writing in 2009. What I know is that the American people demanded change, and elected a President for whom it was a one-word slogan. The country swung hard from right to left, and nothing changed. Military aggression has escalated and expanded. Federal money flows toward corporate cronies faster than ever. The State now surveils us without warrants and detains us without trials. It is clear now that begging the political establishment is not the path to freedom.

Given the hostile rhetoric surrounding Islam's place in American politics, I believe that exploring the natural confluence of values between Muslims and libertarians is more important than ever. As Pastor Martin Niemöller expressed in his famous poem "First they came..." if you do not stand up when the State comes for those most marginalized in society, there will be no one left when they come for you.

As a Muslim, people often ask me if I'm proud to be an American. Basically they want to know, do I pledge allegiance? Well, I don't. I don't stand. I don't place my hand over my heart. I don't speak the words. To me, there is an America in my imagination, the America they taught us about, built on liberty, equality, and justice. But I am heartbroken by the oily nepotism of the real America, which has as little in common with its founding principles as the dollar has with gold, or the statue has with Buddha. The Declaration of Independence states that "Governments are instituted among Men, deriving their just powers from the consent of the governed." I do not consent.

# Chapter One: Islam

## The Standard Disclaimer

First, a warning. Caveat emptor. Buyer beware. Providing an exegesis of Quranic verses is an ambitious task for a layman such as me, and I am unqualified. I firmly believe that civil disagreement is the crucible of Truth, and that reason and evidence are its flame. In that light, logic forces me to take these positions. I consider them Truth, at least until a more convincing argument presents itself, and I invite such evidence. It is my opinion that people should form their own opinions. So, test what I say in the laboratory of your own nervous system, and don't be pointing at me on The Last Day. Everything right and true is from Allah, not from Al Azhar, not from Al Jazeera, not from Al Qaida, but from Allah. If there is wisdom in my words, and those words ring True for you, it is by His Will.

The fundamental and uncompromising keystone of Islam is the belief in the absolute oneness and unity of God. Muslims believe that the religion preached by Jesus Christ is the Truth, that he was the Messiah foretold in the Torah, that he was sent by our Creator as a Mercy to mankind, and that salvation is achieved by following in his path. No Muslim is a Muslim who does not believe this. We accept all His prophets, and His scriptures. We believe in the reality of angels and spirits. We believe that all the affairs of mankind are under His divine decree and one day we are returning to Him to face His merciful assessment of our deeds. We believe this because it is written in the Quran, which we regard as God's final unpolluted revelation, delivered by God's final messenger, the Prophet Muhammad.

# No Compulsion in Religion

> There shall be no compulsion in religion: For Truth has become distinct from error, and whoever rejects falsehood and believes in God has grasped the most trustworthy handhold, which never breaks. And God is Hearing and Knowing.    (Quran 2:256)

The placement of this verse in the Quran is remarkable. It immediately follows The Verse of the Throne, which is the most read, most widely memorized, and most prolifically displayed verse in the Quran. The Verse of the Throne is the John 3:16 of the Quran. So, this statement regarding compulsion is imbedded within potent statements on creed. It was obviously intended to be well known, and therefore well understood. The only published explanations of this verse that I have found are concerned entirely with prohibiting forced conversion. This is a reaction formation to accusations that Islam is spread by the sword. It is not an actionable interpretation by Muslims for Muslims. They do not discuss the implications of prohibiting compulsion in other matters. So, I'd like to decompress the issue as I see it.

The Quran is not careless with language. This sentence is only four words: *La ikrah fi deen*. "No compulsion in religion." Every scholar I've ever heard discuss the word *deen* says that "religion" is a poor translation, and that it means a complete and comprehensive way of life. Why would the Quran use a word that means a complete way of life to describe a principle that only applies to proselytizing? Could it not have said "No compulsion in *dawah*," which literally means "invitation," and is used to describe proselytizing?

The verse is a logical argument. A premise followed by its supporting evidence. The Quran is often constructed in this format. Over and over the Quran tells us, "Will you not use reason?" and that God despises those who don't. "The worst of creatures in the sight of God are the deaf and dumb who do not use their intellect to understand." (Quran 8:22) So, let's break down the argument. Given that Truth is distinct from error, therefore religion must be free from coercion.

Reason dictates that in any instance where the evidence is true, the conclusion must also be true; therefore, when the evidence presented is true in all instances, the premise must be true in all instances. It cannot be true for conversion and false for other matters. How can the premise be abrogated when the supporting evidence remains? This is the principle of non-aggression. "Surely, God loves not the aggressors" (Quran 2:190), i.e., the initiators of coercion.

The principle of non-aggression is a deep and fundamental Truth in human interaction. Actions that are coerced have no moral value. A confession under torture is no real confession. Giving money to the poor at gunpoint is not real charity. The aim of Islam, and religion more broadly, is to place moral value in every action, so how can coercion be virtuous?

The simplicity and profundity of the non-aggression principle is, I believe, the keystone to solving the strife in predominantly Muslim countries, and indeed the world. So, two fundamental questions exist concerning the meaning of this verse: What is compulsion?; and What does it mean that Truth is clear from error? As far as I can tell, the Arabic word *ikrah* is accurately translated as "compulsion" with very little loss of meaning, except that the root word in Arabic is "hatred," which expands the implication. Perhaps "aggression" is a better translation. Compulsion is the use or threat of aggressive force to cause someone to act against their own will. Generally, people consider this the use or threatened use of bodily harm, and some include in this definition threats made to a person's wealth and property.

The Truth is not so clear that people cannot continue to deny and distort it, as they did at the time of this verse. But it is so clear that those who study it and consider it with sincerity often come to believe it, even its most emboldened enemies. This is the fulcrum on which clarity and compulsion turn: sincerity. Compulsion obfuscates sincerity. Therefore sincerity and compulsion must be inversely correlated, and as one waxes, the other must wane. Like oil and water, the two are incompatible.

Let me put it this way: If an Arab flies from Arabia to Malaysia and, the moment he leaves Saudi air space, he has a glass of wine, he doesn't get moral credit for not drinking wine in Arabia, because in his heart of hearts he was abstaining in acquiescence to state aggression, not out of sincere obedience to God. In other words, if you are praying because there is a gun to your head, you are not worshiping God, you are obeying the gunman.

It is my contention that if we carry this verse to its logical extension it means much more than a religion without coercion. A *deen* without coercion means politics without coercion. It means personal relationships without coercion. It means a comprehensive way of life without coercion. So, just as Islamic theology should be characterized by open debate and a free exchange of ideas, an Islamic social order should be characterized by political liberty, and the Muslim family should be characterized by freedom of association.

# Ruminations on a Recent Dream

I had a dream where I was standing on a large stone platform cut into a mountain. On the far side was a rocky slope that went down to a turbulent coast. I stood between two giant floating heads, one in the black Ayatollah turban and the other in the red Al Azhar cap with white turban.

I began asking them questions with the intention of seeking qualified scholarship, but every time, one would tell me the literal meaning of a word in Arabic and the way the ruling was implemented in the early community, and the other would tell me the original intention of the ruling and its application in the modern world. The heads always gave opposite answers, and I was left in the middle with no guidance.

Frustrated, I moved past the heads, toward the ocean. I discovered a wooden stand holding the Quran, and resolved that if I wanted satisfactory answers I'd have to read it for myself—but inside the book I found the pages were not filled with words, just light pouring out. Doubly frustrated, I asked God to teach me how to read.

Then a man appeared, walking up a stairwell that ascended from the ocean. He was all in white, with the same light pouring from his face, so bright that I could not see it. I asked him how to read the light and he answered, "Eat only the purest food. Drink only the purest water. And think only the purest thoughts."

It wasn't exactly English, but more like a raw telepathic communication. It was concise like that, but that's not a perfect translation. I understood that what he meant was to transition slowly into a purer life style by a process of weaning. "Think only the purest thoughts" is a particularly poor translation. The word here translated as "think" contained the digestive implication of "eat" and "drink." It implied that contemplation was a process like digestion, where raw data is separated into valuable information and excrement. The word here translated "thoughts" contained the nutritional implication of "food" and "water." One generally conceives of thoughts as coming from inside, but in this case it suggested ideas taken in from outside, including books, music, radio, television, and even casual conversation. A better translation might be "consume only the purest media."

I lay awake for a long time contemplating. There was a time when dream interpretation was a cherished science in Islam, but books on it are rarely more than symbol dictionaries. My feeling is that dreams are so personal that the meaning must be unique to the individual. Here are my thoughts.

To me the floating heads symbolize the two major flows of thought among Muslims today. The Muslim community is constantly being pulled in two opposing directions, between hard extremism and soft extremism. The scholars who are pulling us apart have metaphorically "lost their heads." They are "not grounded," as it were.

Water is often a symbol of spiritual knowledge. As they say, spirituality without structure is like water without a glass. You'll get yourself wet, but you won't retain anything. This symbol is interesting because "drink the purest water" and "consume the purest media" become synonymous. More significantly, the man in white ascended to the platform from the ocean. I'm fond of saying that Islam is like an infinite ocean, full of pearls and dragons.

In the 13th century Imam Nawawi held a personal conviction not to eat any food harvested from exploitation or oppression. So the literal implementation of the dream may be to eat and drink things which are not only chemically pure, but also morally pure. This is very difficult whem the monetary system itself is a kind of exploitation and oppression. Most of Imam Nawawi's diet was harvested on his own property. So, I did what the Imam did: I started a vegetable garden.

I don't have a yard, only a small apartment balcony. But it was very easy to begin growing. I started with only three rectangular pots where I planted rows of tomatoes, cucumbers, and onions. As they grew I transplanted the small sprouts into larger pots and reseeded the rectangular pots with herbs. Now I have thriving cilantro and chamomile, and soon sage and mint.

It is a uniquely rewarding experience to taste the fruit of your own labor. To put your hands in the soil and dig out a bite of nature. As Thomas Jefferson famously said, "Those who labor in the earth are the chosen people of God, if ever God had a chosen people." Gardening, it turns out, is not a particularly difficult activity either. The materials are inexpensive, the plants are hearty, and I learn as I go. I keep a log of my activities, and have found that taking time out of the day to tend to even a tiny plot of land has been an invaluable opportunity to disconnect and engage in much-needed contemplation.

I cannot recommend this practice enough, even if only with one plant.

# Original Virtue, Not Original Sin

One of the defining events in the Prophet Muhammad's life is called The Night Journey. According to Islamic tradition, Muhammad was taken to Jerusalem by the Angel Gabriel, where he prayed with all the prophets of the past, and then ascended through the seven realms of heaven into the presence of God. It's been described as both a physical and spiritual journey, similar to the ascension narratives in many Eastern religions.

During Muhammad's night journey and ascension, the Angel Gabriel brought him a vessel of wine and a vessel of milk, and asked him to choose. Muhammad chose milk, to which Gabriel said, "You have chosen *fitra*." Common definitions of *fitra* include "innate predisposition" or "primordial nature." This event occurred before any prohibition of alcohol. So, we could interpret that part of *fitra* is an inclination toward right action prior to instruction. It's also interesting to note that milk is the first food we have as infants. So, in part, *fitra* is preserving and trusting our earliest preferences. It is for these reasons that I choose to define *fitra* as "original virtue."

The concept of *fitra* is that God has engraved upon the human soul an inborn tendency toward truth and virtue. It suggests that all human beings are born in a natural state of spiritual purity. This position contradicts both the Doctrine of Original Sin proposed by Christian theology, and the *tabula rasa* proposed by philosophers. Fleshing out the definition requires a look at the Arabic root, and its use in the Quran.

In the Arabic language most nouns are derived from a three-letter root verb. So a book, *kitab*, is literally a thing which is written *ka-ta-ba*. Knowing the root verb often elucidates a deeper understanding of the noun. For *fitra*, the root verb *fa-ta-ra* commonly means to split, or cleave asunder. Less commonly it means to knead and shape like dough, and connotes repetition. Interestingly the verb appears in the Quran eight times, always translated simply as "created," as in "I have set my face, firmly and truly, towards Him Who created the heavens and the earth." (Quran 6:79) One of the divine attributes of God is derived from the same root. *Al Fatir* means The Originator, or the One who creates from nothing. This appears in the Quran six times, as in "Shall I take for my protector any other than God, The Originator of the heavens and the earth?" (Quran 6:14)

So, while mankind possesses original virtue, God is the Originator of virtue. Similarly, we come to see that the meaning of *fitra* is that the reflection of all the divine attributes are inscribed into the human soul, like fingerprints in clay. God is The Merciful, and mankind possesses a predisposition to great mercy. God is The Lover, and mankind possessed a predisposition to great love. God is The Knower, and mankind possesses a predisposition to seek knowledge. God is The Judge, and mankind possesses the capacity for wise judgment. God is The Sovereign, and mankind possesses individual sovereignty. In the Islamic tradition there are 99 divine attributes, and each has a correspondence to an attribute of human nature.

# The Verse of the Sword

> Fight and slay the pagans wherever you find them,
> and seize them, lay siege to them, and lie in wait for
> them in every stratagem of war. (Quran 9:5)

Sounds scary, right? It's known as "The Verse of the Sword," and admittedly many Muslims have used this verse to justify their corrupt intentions. However, it does not establish a doctrine of perpetual violent jihad against all non-Muslims for all time, as the anti-Muslim demagogues would have you believe.

In order to interpret a verse from any scripture, it's important not to ignore the surrounding verses. This alone will be a sufficient rebuttal, but to parse the full intended meaning, it's important to consider the complete context in which it was first revealed. This is especially important with the Quran, because often the verses were given to specific people in specific circumstances that are not actually expressed in the text. The Verse of the Sword appears in the first part of the ninth chapter of the Quran, revealed in the fall of 630 AD in Medina. Here's the context:

Muhammad and the Muslims were driven out of Mecca by torture and boycott, which they patiently and passively endured without violent resistance for years. In 622 they were invited to settle in Yathrib, 200 miles north of Mecca, which became known as Medina.

By 628 the Muslims numbered about 1,400 believers, and Muhammad led a group of them on a pilgrimage to Mecca. Under pre-Islamic tribal custom, all Arabs, regardless of religion, had a right to visit the Kaaba during the pilgrimage months. Also, all the tribes of Arabia observed a pact of non-aggression during those months, and agreed that no blood could be shed within the sanctuary of the Kaaba.

The Muslim pilgrims were halted on the road to Mecca by 200 horsemen from the Quraish, the dominant tribe of Mecca. They were forced to make camp near Hudaibiyah, a small well outside of Mecca. Then Muhammad sent Uthman ibn Affan to assure the tribal chiefs that their intentions were peaceful and to negotiate for permission to make the pilgrimage and leave without incident. The Meccans refused, but agreed to allow the Muslims to make the pilgrimage the following year, so long as their swords remained sheathed and stowed in their bags. They also agreed to a ten-year peace treaty between Mecca and Medina, and affirmed the validity of all private contracts between individuals from either city. Muhammad accepted the terms, against the advice of his companions, and this became known as the Treaty of Hudaibiyah.

Because of the treaty, the Quraish allowed the people of Mecca to visit family members in Medina for the first time in the seven years since the Muslim expulsion from Mecca. As a result, more Meccans accepted Islam in the next two years than during the thirteen years that Muhammad actually preached in Mecca.

Banu Khuzaah, a Bedouin tribe allied with Medina, made camp near the Kaaba during the days permitted by the treaty. During the night they were attacked by the Banu Bakr, a tribe allied with Mecca, and aided with men and arms from the Quraishi chiefs. This attack was a twofold offense. It breached the Treaty of Hudaibiyah, but also it breached the tribal traditions, which held that war could not be waged in the sacred months, and that blood could not be shed in the holy sanctuary. Once word of this reached Muhammad, he offered the chiefs of the Quraish three options: the first was to pay restitution to the families of the Banu Khuzaah who had been killed; the second was to disassociate from Banu Bakr and turn them out of Mecca; the third was to break the treaty and declare war with the Muslims. The Quraish accepted the third, and preparations were made for war.

This verse was revealed in the final portion of the sacred months, after war had been declared, but before any battle had occurred. So, let's look again. But this time, we'll also read the surrounding verses:

> The treaties are not dissolved with those pagans with whom ye have entered into alliance and who have not subsequently failed you, nor aided any one against you. So fulfill your engagements with them to the end of their term: for God loves the righteous. (Quran 9:4)

It could not be more obvious that this does not apply to *all* pagans. Those pagans who honored their agreement were not involved. It is only directed toward the Banu Bakr who violated the treaty, and the Quraishi chiefs who aided them. To all other pagans, this verse affirms the pact through to the end of the term, which is the remaining eight years of the treaty.

And then the big scary line:

> But when the sacred months are past, then fight and slay the pagans wherever ye find them, and seize them, lay siege to them, and lie in wait for them in every stratagem of war. But if they repent, and establish regular prayers and practice regular charity, then open the way for them: for God is Oft-forgiving, Most Merciful. (Quran 9:5)

The instructions are clear. They were to obey the tradition prohibiting war during the sacred months. Once the months were past, they were to march on Mecca, targeting those pagans who'd initiated the aggression, and honoring the non-aggression pact with everyone else. Many among the anti-Muslim demagogues have argued that this is calling for forced conversion. This interpretation doesn't really fit, considering it was the Banu Bakr who initiated the aggression—but the next verse removes all doubt:

> If one amongst the pagans asks you for asylum,
> grant it to him, so that he may hear the word of God;
> and then escort him to where he can be secure.
> That is because they are men without knowledge.
> (Quran 9:6)

The way the Quran presents options is by describing the best case scenario first, and less preferable but equally acceptable options in succession. So, if an individual among the Banu Bakr repents and accepts Islam, this is ideal. But even if they just cease aggression and ask for protection, amnesty should be given to them. Not only should they be protected, they should be escorted out of the battle to a place of safety.

Regardless of what people today say it means, this is how the Muslims understood it at the time. Muhammad had so much success in Medina and with the surrounding tribes that when the time came to march, they had become an army of 10,000. Abu Sufyan, the leader of the Quraish, went to Muhammad to negotiate and was told to go into Mecca and tell everyone that they would be safe. The Muslims only attacked the neighborhood of the Banu Bakr, who assailed them with arrows, and were eventually killed. One report says thirteen men were killed, the other says twenty-eight. Two Muslims were killed in both accounts. This was not a massacre by any measure. Under tribal law, and the terms of the treaty, the Muslims had every right to wage a full assault on all of Mecca, but Muhammad limited the attack to those who initiated the aggression.

There are some basic principles that I think we can derive from this story. Keep in mind, you're free to form your own opinion.

### 1) The primacy of achieving peace over demanding rights:
Prophet Muhammad agreed to the Treaty of Hudaibiyah against the advice of his companions. The incident at Hudaibiyah could have exposed the contradiction of the Quraishi policy toward the Muslims. If they had escalated the situation into a physical confrontation, the Quraish would have lost reputation with the Meccan tribes for violating their own law. But if they had permitted the Muslims to make the pilgrimage, they would have lost reputation with the Meccan tribes for acquiescing to Muhammad. By pressing forward to the Kaaba, the Muslims would have won a blow against Quraishi either way.

Muhammad had the upper hand simply by demanding their tribal rights, but either outcome would have increased animosity and potentially escalated hostility. The promise of ten years of peace outweighed the escalation of aggression to secure tribal rights.

### 2) The supremacy of contract law:

Contract law can be summarized very simply in seven words: "Do all that you agree to do." Whether by oath or by written agreement, it is incumbent on every righteous person of any creed to live by their word. The Treaty of Hudaibiyah affirmed the validity of all private contracts, which indicates to me that rival municipal authorities have no right to interfere with the supremacy of private contracts. Individuals must be allowed to live by their word without political interference. But the political order must also live by its word. The treaty itself is a contract between Mecca and Medina, and violating that contract justified the use of force. Therefore, enforcing contract law, and holding people at any level of society accountable for their oaths and written agreements is a legitimate use of force.

### 3) The superiority of restorative justice over punitive justice:

There are two theories of justice symbolized by the sword and scales in secular iconography. Punitive justice, symbolized by the sword, is an approach where statutory law is enforced through punishment. Restorative justice, symbolized by the scales, is an approach where the focus is upon making the victim whole again. Offenders are made to take responsibility for their actions by repairing the damage they have done. In this theory of justice, reparation rather than punishment takes a central role. Remember, when options are given in a series, the first option is the ideal. The first option Muhammad offered to the Quraish was to pay restitution to the families of the Banu Khuzaah who were killed. So, we can deduce that restorative justice is preferable to punitive justice, and the primary role of justice, even at an international level, is to make the victim at the individual level whole again, not to pay an abstract debt to society at large.

### 4) The Non-Aggression Principle:

The Non-Aggression Principle holds that the initiation of physical force, threat, or fraud is always illegitimate, and that the use of force is only appropriate when used in defense. This is the defining lesson of this story, and the criterion for determining between the times when physical violence is legitimate and those when patient passive endurance is appropriate. Even when the terms of a treaty authorize him, and the customs of the society permit him, Muhammad does not use physical force against anyone unless they have first aggressed, or supplied an aggressor with material aid.

# Apostasy: An Unqualified Fatwa

It is a widely accepted misconception that the Quran calls for the death penalty for apostasy. This is mostly claimed by anti-Muslim demagogues, and it's utterly false. No such verse exists, and I challenge them to cite one. The Quran speaks repeatedly of people returning to disbelief after believing, but never says they should be punished in this life. Let's take a look:

> How shall God guide those who reject faith after they accepted it and bore witness that the Messenger was true and that clear signs had come unto them? God guides not a people unjust. —For such the reward is that on them rests the curse of God, and His angels. (Quran 3:86-87)

No death penalty there.

> Those who believe, then reject faith, then believe again and again, reject faith, and go on increasing in disbelief, God will not forgive them nor guide them nor guide them on the way. (Quran 4:137)

Maybe you can explain to me how a person enters Islam, and then leaves it, then enters again, and then leaves it again... if you're supposed to kill them when they left the first time.

> Anyone who, after accepting faith in God, utters disbelief, except under compulsion, his heart remaining firm in Faith, but such as open their heart to disbelief, on them is wrath from God, and theirs will be a dreadful penalty. —This is because they love the life of this world better than the hereafter: and God will not guide those who reject faith. —Those are they whose hearts, ears, and eyes God has sealed, and they take no heed. —Without doubt, in the hereafter they will perish. (Quran 16:106-109)

So, the "dreadful penalty" for apostasy is God's to bring in the hereafter.

The only time the Quran ever says anything about killing apostates, it is in reference to a specific event in the life of Muhammad. While the Muslims were in Mecca, there was great persecution at the hands of the pagans, and the Quran spoke at length about hypocrites among the Muslims who were spies from the pagans. Then the Muslims fled Mecca and migrated to Medina. This migration revealed the hypocrites, because they refused to leave Mecca. So, permission was given to fight those who joined pagan tribes in aggressing against the Muslims.

> They desire that you should reject faith, as they do, that you may be like them. So, take not friends from among them until they flee in the way of God (to Medina). But if they turn back (to Mecca), seize them and kill them wherever you find them, and take not friends nor helpers from among them. —Except those who join a people with whom you have a treaty of peace, or those who approach you with hearts restraining them from fighting you or fighting their own people. Had God willed He would have given them power over you, and they would have fought you. Therefore if they withdraw from you, but fight you not, and offer you peace, then God has opened no way for you to war against them. (Quran 4:89-91)

In this passage the apostates are broken into three categories:
1) Those allied with a tribe that has a peace treaty with the Muslims.
2) Those who wish to remain neutral in the conflict.
3) Those allied with a tribe engaged in open hostilities towards the Muslims.

As everywhere else in the Quran, permission is only given to fight those who aggressed on you first. And this verse clearly prohibits Muslims from fighting those who leave Islam if they wish to live in peace or neutrality. I'm not sure how much clearer "no way for you to war against them" can be.

But then we get that famous hadith, favorite of Robert Spencer, Pamela Geller, and all the anti-Muslim demagogues:
Whoever changes his religion, kill him.

Whoa! Well that's problematic, isn't it? It seems perfectly clear: kill the apostates, right? Heck, it means kill the converts too! The hadith are not Quranic scripture. They are the actions and sayings of Muhammad as recorded by his companions, and by successive generations. As a result, they all have varying levels of reliability. Well, this hadith is unreliable for a number of reasons. First we've got to read the whole thing:

> Narrated by Ikrima: Some atheists were brought to Ali and he burnt them. The news of this event, reached Ibn Abbas who said, "If I had been in his place, I would not have burnt them, as Allah's Apostle forbade it, saying, "Do not punish anybody with God's punishment (fire)." I would have killed them according to the statement of God's Apostle, "Whoever changed his religion, kill him." (Bukhari Volume 9, Book 84, Number 57)

Unlike the Gospels, where a council of bishops decided which accounts of Jesus' life they thought were authentic and destroyed those they felt were not, accounts of Muhammad's life are all recorded in hundreds of volumes, but each narration contains a chain of custody describing in detail who gave the account. These chains are used to determine the strength of the narration. So, narrations with long chains are weaker than those with short chains. Narrations reported by many independent witnesses are stronger than those with only one witness. And sometimes the lack of credibility of a particular narrator can cast doubt on an entire chain.

This hadith appears, with minor variations, in most of the major hadith collections (Bukhari, Tirmidhi, Abu Dawud and Ibn Majah), but always with the same chain of narration. The hadith is narrated only by Ikrima in the second generation, and only by Ibn Abbas in the first generation. The only person in the chain who ever met Muhammad is Ibn Abbas, who was 10 years old when he converted and 13 when Muhammad died. Further, examining the reliability of the narrators, you'll find that many scholars considered Ikrima a liar, or at the very least untrustworthy, because he was known to despise Ali.

So, to believe that this was an authentic teaching from Muhammad, you'd have to believe that he gave a law prescribing the death penalty to a child, and no one else, not even Ali, who had been his companion for twenty-three years. And you'd have to believe that the boy tells no one except a liar. This is how the law is transmitted. But it's not even transmitted well. In this narration the word for atheists is *Zanadiqa*, which is not Arabic, but Persian. In another it says, "those who abandoned Islam," and in another it says, "people from al-Zatt who worshiped idols." These narrations of the same event are irreconcilable. An atheist cannot be an idol worshiper. It's far easier for me to believe that Ikrima invented this out of whole cloth to discredit Ali.

This becomes obvious if you read the same hadith in the collection of Abu Dawud, which ends differently:

> Ayyub informed us from Ikrima that Ali, peace be upon him, burned some people who abandoned

Islam. This reached Ibn Abbas and he said: "I would not have burnt them with fire. Indeed, the Messenger of God said: 'Do not punish with the punishment of God.' I would have killed them in accordance with the word of the Messenger of God. For, surely the Messenger of God said: 'Whoever changed his religion kill him.' " This reached Ali, peace be upon him, and he said: "Woe to Ibn Abbas." (Abu Da`ud 3787)

It's a hadith about a rumor that Ali had been burning apostates, which never actually happened, or at least was not recorded anywhere else. And when the rumor reached Ali, he says "woe" to the person spreading the rumor. Ibn Abbas was vindicated later, however. It was reported by Abdullah bin al-Harith that when he visited Ali, he was shocked to find Ikrima bound to a post outside the door of Ali's house. When he asked Ali regarding this, Ali explained by saying: "This wicked man attributes false sayings to Ibn Abbas." This hadith is now what it was then... a vicious rumor.

Unfortunately the misconception that the punishment for apostasy is death is common, even among Muslims. In reality this ruling comes from an age when apostasy and treason were synonymous. Indeed, to convert to Christianity in a Muslim country at the height of the Crusades would have likely cost you your head. Robert Spencer and the anti-Muslim demagogues like to oversimplify this historic opinion by implying that it is unanimous across all scholars, but this is simply false. There has always been a difference of opinion, and most scholars, most notably Ibn Taymiyyah, draw a distinction between minor apostasy and major apostasy. Minor apostasy, which consists only of leaving Islam, carries no punishment, while major apostasy, which includes some kind of espionage or treason, deserved punishment.

Muslims who continue to defend this ruling typically argue that it is a deterrent from apostasy. Nothing could be further from the truth. If anything, the existence of the ruling makes Islam difficult to accept. Sincere belief is a response to evidence. It is not possible to impartially consider evidence under the threat of death. Using a physical deterrent against a mental posture is impossible. This can only produce hypocrisy. You can't will yourself to believe, you can only will yourself to behave.

The appeal to authority, where it is argued that a hadith is strong because Imam Bukhari said it was strong; is a logical fallacy. The leaders of every school of Islamic jurisprudence knew this, which is why they all made statements to the effect that they were fallible, and their opinions were subject to evidence and not to be followed blindly.

In Islam we call our methodologies *sciences*. For example, "the science of hadith." A science, by definition, requires a method of inquiry based upon measurable evidence, subject to specific principles of reasoning, which produces results that can be validated through replication. In the science of hadith, narrations are measured based upon the strength of their chain. So, given the same evidence, and the same principles, we should be able to duplicate the results of previous scholars. We should be able to come to the same conclusion they did. But we can't. Not with this hadith.

As I discussed previously, actions which are coerced have no moral value. What greater coercive force is there than the threat of death? It is a basic principle in Islam that you should be strict with yourself, and soft with others. If there is any difference of opinion, we are supposed to give others the benefit of the more lenient position. If even one scholar disagrees with such a ruling, that is doubt enough to never enforce it. I stand with Muhammad's wife Aisha, who said, "It is preferable to pardon mistakenly than to punish mistakenly."

> The worst of creatures in the sight of Allah are the deaf and dumb who do not use their intellect to understand. (Quran 8:22)

# Empathy Day

For those in the West, gender equality is a huge stumbling block on the road to understanding Islam. This may be in part because US history is inseparably tied to the history of slavery, segregation, and the doctrine of "separate but equal."

Children in school today are taught that "separate but equal is not equal," a phrase from the landmark Supreme Court decision *Oliver Brown* v. *Topeka Board of Education* (1954), which overturned the Constitutionality of racial segregation as a violation of the Equal Protection Clause of the US Constitution. This victory opened the door to the Civil Rights and Women's Liberation movements of the 1960s.

To Americans, especially those concerned with civil rights, when men and women are separated in the mosque, it immediately triggers concerns about gender equality, which is exacerbated by the high instances of domestic violence and the clear denial of civil rights to women in the Muslim-majority countries. So, naturally, they presume Islam is the problem, even though to Muslims, Islam prescribes a comprehensive system of rights and responsibilities for men and women that may not be identical, but should be complementary. Not to put too strong a point on it, but if you are one of these guys who beats his wife, you ought to be ashamed of yourself. What you are doing is evil, and the fact that you are contributing to our community being characterized by domestic violence is despicable. If you want my opinion, you should be begging her forgiveness, preferably in public.

While the primary symptom is a denial of women's rights, specifically those guaranteed to them by Islam, I feel the primary problem is a lack of empathy. Although many people mistakenly believe them to be synonymous, *empathy* and *sympathy* have very distinct meanings. While sympathy connotes a kind of pity or compassion for a person, it doesn't mean you really understand what it's like to be in their situation. Empathy is a level above that where you are actually capable of feeling what the other person is feeling vicariously. To make it easy to remember, sympathy is feeling *for* someone, empathy is feeling *with* someone. For most people, actual empathy is very difficult to achieve without having some measure of similar experience. I have a proposal to rectify that deficiency.

If your local mosque is like most mosques, men and women pray in separate rooms. Do not assume for a moment that this wall of separation is from the teachings of the Prophet. I will dispel that in an instant.

Abu Hurairah reported that the Messenger of Allah said:
The best rows for men are the first rows, and the worst ones the last ones, and the best rows for women are the last ones and the worst ones for them are the first ones. (Sahih Muslim 4:881)

The only way this hadith makes any sense is if men and women are praying in the same room, and in the same rows. The walls we place between men and women are completely inappropriate. It is an innovation and an injustice.

We have to deal with reality before we can implement the solution, and the reality is, men and women pray in separate rooms in most mosques—and in the vast majority of mosques, women have much poorer facilities than men. I sympathize with my sisters, believe me. But I would rather *empathize*, and if my brothers will join me, I have an idea how.

I imagine an event where the men sit in the women's room and the women sit in the men's room. An event where women may go to the mosque and worship in huge halls while men are crowded together into back rooms. An event where women can sit and read the Quran and offer prayers in peace while men contend with hyperactive children and screaming babies.

I imagine an event where the most knowledgeable women in the community ascend the minbar and deliver lectures on the rights of women in Islam while men sit behind the wall and listen through an intermittent sound system. An event where sisters gather around, free to voice their questions and their concerns while the men pass their questions forward on hand-written notes.

I imagine an event where women sit around and sip tea and socialize while men prepare the meal.

Obviously some considerations must be taken into account. Some provisions must be made to assure that valid congregational prayers can be made. Also, obviously the women of the community should be the primary organizers of such an event to ensure that their unique concerns are expressed. I'm sure there are plenty of issues that men have no idea are problems in their community. And finally, I think a round table meeting at the end of the event, when everyone can discuss their reactions together, is crucial to the successful achievement of authentic empathy.

Now, I'm sure there are male readers who are uncomfortable with this suggestion. But realize, the degree to which you are uneasy is exactly the degree to which there is injustice to the women in your community. The degree to which you would object to this experience for one day is exactly the degree to which the women in your community object to this treatment every day. Even if such an event never takes place, if you examine your emotional reaction to the suggestion, you'll have some idea how your sisters feel. And even though it may be uncomfortable in the short term, in the long term, if we can have more empathy for one another, we will be more inclined to fulfill each other's rights, and we will live with greater peace and tranquility for all involved.

# Is Libertarianism Compatible With Islam?

I came across an article on LewRockwell.com titled "Is Libertarianism Compatible With Religion?" in which author Laurence M. Vance reflected that he, a devout Christian, and Murray Rothbard, an agnostic Jew, would have gotten along because they shared a common enemy in the State. I have often said that the amazing thing to me about liberty is that it can put atheists and Muslims on the same team. But as Vance levied a wall of Biblical verses to bolster his thesis that freedom unified people of diverse faiths, I saw the need for such an article written from an Islamic perspective. It seems that answering this question may turn out to be my life's pursuit, which makes these first awkward steps that much more difficult—but let's take a running start at it and see how far it takes us.

Polling data suggests that Muslims comprise 1 to 2% of the American population. Libertarian candidates rarely exceed 1% of the vote in any presidential race (although many libertarians throw their support behind liberty-minded Republicans like Ron Paul, or don't vote at all, like myself). Still, if these numbers are any indication, the odds of me meeting another American Muslim libertarian should be a statistical anomaly. Yet dozens of my friends and acquaintances place themselves somewhere on the libertarian spectrum, from libertarian partyarchs to full-blown anarcho-capitalists and all points in between. Although this observation certainly is not scientific by any measure, to me it does suggest a confluence of values that is seldom examined.

I am in good company in this pursuit. Legal professor John A. Makdisi makes the case that the origins of common law are to be traced to the Maliki school of Islamic jurisprudence in North Africa. Anthropologist Spencer MacCallum has argued that the same legal tradition has allowed Somalia to exist in virtual anarchy since 1991 and even prosper relative to their living conditions prior to dismantling the State. Rose Wilder Lane, regarded as one of the founding mothers of the libertarian movement, wrote "Islam and the Discovery of Freedom," in which she describes early Islamic civilization as a virtually stateless society that flourished because of its emphasis on free markets and individual rights. She credits Muslim traders and scholars with introducing the West to liberty, especially the idea of individual conscience.

A great hurdle that many have toward understanding and accepting the philosophy of libertarianism is the misperception that libertarians advocate drug use, sexual promiscuity, gambling, and other vices, the suppression of which dominate the political platforms of social conservatives. In reality the philosophy of libertarianism has no position on these activities, and whether or not any particular libertarian advocates or discourages them is a matter of individual opinion. What libertarianism is is a political philosophy that defines the appropriate role of violence in society.

Ask yourself this question: "Do I believe violence should be used to solve non-violent problems?"

If you answered "No," you are a libertarian. If you answered "Yes," you are an authoritarian. Everything else is just learning to apply that answer consistently.

Libertarianism holds that the only appropriate use of violence is in defense of one's person or property against aggression, and that the initiation of violence is unacceptable and damaging to society. So, for example, I don't smoke cannabis, and I discourage people from using it without a medical cause, but I certainly cannot advocate the use of violence to prevent people from using cannabis, which is a non-violent act. This is known as the non-aggression principle, which is the cornerstone of the libertarian philosophy.

One doesn't have to look far to find the non-aggression principle in the Quran. The verse "There shall be no coercion in religion" (Quran 2:256), with the word *deen* (here translated as "religion") understood to mean a complete and comprehensive way of life, immediately follows The Verse of the Throne, which is one of the most read, most widely memorized and most prolifically displayed verses in the whole Quran. So, this prohibition of coercion is inseparably linked with one of the Quran's most potent statements of creed. For Christians it would be as if the verse were found at John 3:17 in the Bible.

The non-aggression principle is a deep and self-evident Truth in human interaction. Actions that are coerced have no moral value. So if the aim of Islam, and religion more broadly, is to fill every action with virtue, coercion can never achieve this. A person behaving virtuously while under compulsion lacks inward sincerity, and therefore virtue. Compulsion and sincerity are incompatible and must be inversely correlated. As one waxes, the other must wane. You cannot achieve authentic virtue by threatening the cannabis smoker with violence—you can only inculcate hypocrisy.

What does this mean for the State?

Carried to its logical conclusion, a *deen* without coercion is also a political order without coercion, which is no State at all by current definitions. In modern political science jargon, a "nation state" is an institution that claims the monopoly privilege to initiate violence to achieve sociopolitical goals. If you consistently apply the non-aggression principle, you can't have a State by this definition. But it's hard to imagine a robust libertarian tradition in Islam when one looks at what centuries of authoritarianism have wrought in predominantly

Muslim countries. You must go further back, to the foundations upon which Muhammad built the social order in Medina.

The society in Medina was pluralistic, accommodating a diversity of tribes, many of which were Jewish and Pagan. In the West, pluralism was achieved by taking monopoly privilege away from the Church and giving it to the State. Yet, today we still find power used to oppress the powerless. The problem is monopoly itself. You cannot protect pluralism, which is mandated in the Quran, with a monopoly.

The social order in Medina was called a *mithaq*, which is a covenant between independent parties. It's closer to the word "union" than "State." Tribal groups enjoyed self-determination as separate units in society. Muslims made up one unit in which Islamic law was observed, but each of the Jewish and Pagan tribes were recognized as independent and free to practice their own religion, to form their own judicial system, and observe their own laws, not Islamic law. These independent units formed a union only to the extent that they negotiated a written Constitutional agreement outlining a mutual protection pact to defend against outside aggression, and a non-aggression pact to prohibit attacks from within.

For the Constitutionalist Muslim the similarity between this union and the American union is sufficient to consider oneself a libertarian in the American political system. The only role of the State becomes protection from enemies foreign and domestic. But for Muslims who desire to consistently apply the non-aggression principle to the State itself, another step must be taken. One must ask how Muhammad's authority was legitimized. Most Muslims will say that Muhammad's authority as a leader came from God, which is a fine answer for a Muslim, but not for the Jews and Pagans of Medina. In Medina's social order, authority was derived from *bayah*, which literally means "to sell." It is a pledge of allegiance or social contract. Bayah in Muhammad's time was an explicit voluntary arrangement, not a coercive one. It was a contract between individuals outlining mutual rights and responsibilities, not arbitrary authority to enforce sociopolitical preferences through violence.

So, Islamic political theory has all the same baggage as Western thought around "consent of the governed." Like the West, early Islamic scholars developed a doctrine of "tacit consent" where social contracts were not a function individuals entered voluntarily, but were instead tied to land and borders. In short, the State—love it or leave it. But there is no denying that this was not the social order in Medina. Pagans, Jews, and Muslims shared the same roads, traded in the same markets, and drank from the same wells. They were part of different social spheres, sharing no obligations to each other except those they contracted. Legal systems were not separated by territorial boundaries, as States are today. They existed right on top of one another, shifting according to consent, not jurisdiction.

After Muhammad died, the Muslims did the same thing that Americans did after winning their independence—they prioritized unity over consent, and it had the same results: civil war. If you prioritize unity over consent, you can only manufacture tacit consent with violence, leading to an ever-increasing need for authoritarianism. Because, just as violence cannot achieve authentic virtue, violence cannot achieve authentic unity—it can only inculcate hypocrisy. But if you go back and consistently apply the non-aggression principle, and you prioritize consent over unity, you will allow the emergence of a more peaceful, more diverse, more libertarian *deen*.

# Islam and the Discovery of Freedom

I read the entirety of "Islam and the Discovery of Freedom" by Rose Wilder Lane on a direct flight from San Francisco to New Hampshire. I literally cried as she chronicled the great liberty of the past being eclipsed by tyranny. In my heart I found a new love for my friend and teacher Imam Suhaib Webb, whose Islamic literacy class gave me the tools necessary to better grasp the meaning of the commentary by Dr. Imad-ad-Deen Ahmad.

Born in 1886, Rose Wilder Lane is regarded as one of the founding mothers of the libertarian movement. Her book *The Discovery of Freedom: Man's Struggle Against Authority* is said to have been written from beginning to end in "a white heat" and consequently contains numerous historical (but not philosophical) errors. Dissatisfied, and perhaps embarrassed, by these errors, Lane withdrew it from publication, but in her wisdom she devoted a chapter to Islam's contributions to the philosophy of liberty. Now that chapter is available with commentary provided by Dr. Imad-ad-Deen Ahmad of the Minaret of Freedom Institute. He corrects her minor historical and theological errors, but further bolsters her thesis that the golden age of Islamic civilization was the product of its abundant liberty, and its downfall was the result of its decline into tyranny.

Lane begins by summarizing Abraham's message as, "there is only one God, who has blessed mankind with freewill. They bear accountability for their righteous or evil actions. The pagan gods do not exist, and do not control the affairs of mankind." She regards this as the first great attempt to liberate mankind from illegitimate authority, and describes history as a struggle between this conviction, that human beings are self-controlling and individually responsible, and attempts by earthly authorities to make themselves into false gods over mankind.

She regards Muhammad's message as the second great attempt to establish liberty on Earth. I found her description of the Prophet as a practical, humorous, friendly business executive to be utterly refreshing. In Muhammad's view, according to Lane, priests corrupted the pure message of Abraham, Moses, and Jesus when they assumed authority to control mankind. It was therefore incumbent upon mankind to establish a direct relationship to God without priests. This recognition of mankind as individually volitional beings laid the foundation for what Lane calls the world's first scientific civilization in the modern sense. She writes, "whenever authority was weak, men opened schools of science," because in the Islamic world view there was no distinction between sacred and profane knowledge. All Truth is from God.

Lane describes the earliest Islamic universities as marketplaces of knowledge like the bazaars. Men of knowledge came to sell their instruction in open forum, and students were free to wander about listening. When they decided upon a teacher, they met privately to establish a curriculum and agree upon fees. These universities were privately funded and virtually without State regulation. They were regulated by reputation. A teacher's success or failure hinged upon the market demand for the knowledge he sold. If the student was dissatisfied, he simply left to find another teacher, and when he'd had his fill of education, he left school to apply his knowledge.

Lane writes, "Europeans were not able to impose upon that university any tinge of the European belief that minds acquire knowledge, not by actively seeking to know, but by passively being taught whatever Authority decides that they should know." The result was an explosion of human energy that led to advanced mathematics, medicine, chemistry, astronomy, cosmetics, hygiene, art, and philosophy that appeared like utter magic to medieval Europeans.

Beyond schools, there were also hospitals, libraries, paved roads, and whole water irrigation networks built and maintained by similar private foundations. All institutions and infrastructure that might characterize an advanced civilization were produced without State intervention. Even law was developed by scholars independent of government. Law was not legislated, but discovered the same way that natural scientists discover the laws of physical, chemical, and biological systems. A judge, or *qadi*, was independent of the State. To keep his reputation for wisdom, he had to find ways to settle disputes that satisfied everyone's sense of justice. No single organization, religious, social, or political, extended over the whole civilization. No monopoly means no State by modern definitions.

Lane makes the argument, quite effectively in fact, that through Italy the Muslims gave Europe the enlightenment, and through Spain the Muslims gave Europe the maps, the navigational tools, and the love for freedom that drove them to the New World. In Muslim Spain, generations of European Christians and Jews experienced freedom of thought and conscience unprecedented anywhere else in Europe. In the century after Granada fell and Spain returned to Catholic rule, the Spaniards were less submissive to government than any other Europeans, and it was during that century that Spaniards explored and conquered the New World. Lane suggests it was the love of freedom learned from the Muslims that drove free-thinking Europeans away from tyranny and across the Atlantic Ocean.

Most Muslims fled to Muslim lands, but those who stayed in Spain were forced to convert to Catholicism and came to be called *Moriscos*. There was doubt about the sincerity of their conversion when they persisted in their Islamic customs such as reading... and bathing. The State responded by burning libraries, and prohibiting the Moriscos from bathing secretly in their homes. The Spanish Inquisition began in large part to expose secret Muslims in Spain, and uncover the "Apostasies and Treasons of the Moriscos." In 1602, among the charges against the Moriscos was that they "commended nothing so much as that liberty of conscience in all matters of religion, which the Turks and all other Mohammedans suffer their subjects to enjoy." What the investigation found was that freedom of thought, skepticism of government, and passion for freedom had infected Spaniards who had never been Muslim. So, naturally, those Christians accustomed to this freedom, who could not abide such religious persecution, fled to the New World.

According to Lane, Muslims "forgot the God of Abraham" sometime in the 16th century, and rejected the personal responsibility of freedom. Islamic civilization began to resemble the rest of Europe as a static society of controlling authority. But the mantle of liberty had been passed to the Americans directly from the Muslims in Spain. Lane regards the American Revolution as the third and most current attempt to establish a free society on Earth, where political conditions would not hinder mankind's natural inclination toward scientific progress.

Many Muslims will speak of the Islamic golden age as an invitation to non-Muslims to challenge their stereotypes of Islam. This is not my aim. I intend to look to this glorious past and imagine what progress we are capable of if only we demand the freedom from tyranny they had in those days. Unfortunately, Lane offers virtually no explanation for why the Muslim world changed. But if we're ever to reclaim the liberty we have lost, it's important that we don't try to manage the symptoms and instead diagnose the disease. It's important that we acknowledge that the success of the past was not achieved by central authority, but by living in conditions where human energy was free from control.

# Voluntary Islam: Separation of Everything and State

When I describe what I am advocating as, "no State by current definitions," it causes much anxiety for some people. It's understandable, and I feel I owe people an explanation of what a stateless Islamic society might look like.

To understand what is meant by "no State by current definitions," we must of course examine the definition of "State" itself, which, as discussed previously, is "an entity that claims a monopoly on violence in a given geographical area." This definition is widely accepted by most modern political scientists, and was even cited by Senator Barack Obama in an interview with the *Military Times* editorial board in 2008. Of course, this is fundamentally identical to the definition of *terrorism*, which is "the use or threat of coercive violence against civilians to achieve political or ideological goals."

Now, asking me to predict what a society would look like without a violent monopoly is a bit like asking an abolitionist how blacks in the South would all find jobs without slavery, or asking a capitalist exactly how many loaves of bread to stock in each Russian grocery if they abandon communism. No individual person or organization can possibly predict or satisfy all the needs of free people. To even ask the question presumes that an individual can know the answer. But we can be confident that free people find brilliant and innovative ways to solve social problems. We can also be confident that this model of organizing society through centrally planned violence is irredeemably insolvent and must collapse. That which is economically unsustainable cannot endure. The advent of a free society is entirely inevitable. So, we would be wise to prepare for it.

The central claim of Statism is that a monopoly on violence is the best strategy for providing public services and settling legal disputes. Any objective look at history immediately reveals that the only thing the State succeeds at is increasing its own power.

Let's imagine if the Muslim world had no monopoly on violence, and the population needed a new social structure. If the Prophet Muhammad were trying to structure such a society from scratch, he would likely begin as he did in Medina, with the *mithaq,* a non-aggression pact between the Muslim and non-Muslim populations. A non-aggression pact is not a monopoly on violence—in fact, it's almost the opposite, because a State is by definition an aggressive organization. Second, a mutual protection pact to defend each other from outside aggression. A mutual protection pact is still not a monopoly on violence—in fact, if anything, it's a decentralization of the capacity for violence. Finally, Muhammad served as an arbiter of disputes between diverse tribes. This is the closest thing to a State in Medina under Muhammad's direction, but he had no power to legislate outside the Muslim community. The non-Muslim tribes of Medina had their own private judiciaries and lived by their own legal systems.

There's just one problem. In those days there was one Muslim community, organized under a single leader. It's a beautiful ideal, but today it's simply not a reality. The Muslim world is lousy with tyrants who will never voluntarily relinquish their violent monopolies. The strategy of most Islamic movements today consists of elevating a single interpretation, usually an unreasonably strict and wildly impractical interpretation, and then attempting to seize the reins of the violent monopoly so they can impose their interpretation on the masses. Uniformity is not unity. Authentic unity can never be achieved through compulsion, as we've discussed previously.

The solution is that Muslims be allowed the same rights non-Muslims had in Medina, the right to form private judiciaries and establish their own decentralized legal systems. Traditionally, authority in Islamic society was derived from *bayah*, which literally means "to sell." It's a pledge of allegiance to a leader. Without a violent monopoly it would become an act of explicit consent, as it was in Muhammad's lifetime, and not the tacit consent of violent monopolies today. Muslims could voluntarily choose the leaders, private judiciaries, and legal systems that most reflected their views. Because there is no regional monopoly, borders disappear. Leaders and judiciaries would be forced to compete for the *bayah* of their adherents. Those espousing legal systems that were unconvincing or impractical would quickly find their followers leaving them for those who brought the best evidence and demonstrated the best justice.

For example, those Muslims who wished to treat the problem of alcoholism through lashing, as some violent monopolies do to this day, would be free to form organizations that imposed those rules on them. And to some degree, the fact that their adherents explicitly consented to the rule softens the horror for the rest of us. Similarly, those Muslims who desired alternative treatments for alcoholism (rehabilitation, pharmaceuticals, hypnosis, etc.) would be free to experiment. Each organization would develop a track record and a reputation for its strategies for solving social problems. Anyone seeking treatment for alcoholism would not only have options, but hard data to help them choose the more likely treatment to succeed.

What about those addicted to this mad fantasy that their political weakness is due to the lack of uniformity of religious opinion? Getting all Muslims in one tent is not impossible in this model. It just has to happen organically. In fact, I'd argue that it is easier to achieve this way than by force. To form a unified Muslim community independent of violent monopolies, they'd need to form an umbrella organization that began soliciting the consent of all private judiciaries. What they would quickly realize is that the more people they tried to include, the less they'd be able to do, because they would lack agreement.

In the old model (or, I guess, the current model) those of divergent opinion are forced to obey the opinion of the group with superior force. This has never produced uniformity or agreement in history. In the new model, an umbrella organization would either have to broaden their interpretation to include the divergent viewpoints, or allow them to form their own organization. The broadest agreement you really need to form a coherent and functional society is the *mithaq* itself, a pact of non-aggression. Indeed anyone who could not abide by this simple principle is by definition a violent aggressive element and should have no place in society anyway.

# Ninth-Century Muslim Anarchists

I came across an article titled "Ninth-Century Muslim Anarchists" by Patricia Crone, scholar of early Islamic history at the Institute for Advanced Study, Princeton, which centers around a discussion that was taking place in Basra in southern Iraq in the 800s. There was a general consensus that the Abbasid Caliphate, which controlled a vast empire from Baghdad, had become corrupt and tyrannical. So the question among the scholars became how the community should respond to a leader who had become "all too reminiscent of Pharaoh," as Crone puts it. This article was originally published in 2000 in the *Past & Present* journal. But in light of the Arab Spring, I think it's valuable to pick up the discussion where they left off.

The mainstream opinions are broadly categorized as activists and quietists by Crone. The activists held that when a leader lost legitimacy, it was obligatory to stage a violent revolution and install a new legitimate leader. The quietists held that civil war was worse than oppression and it was obligatory to patiently persevere under tyranny. You had to obey the tyrant, or at the most, resist passively. For whatever reason, the quietist position has been and remains the dominant position, even though it contradicts the opinion of Muhammad's companion Abu Bakr, who said upon his inauguration, "Obey me as long as I obey God and His Prophet. But if I disobey God's command or His Prophet, then no obedience is incumbent upon you." The quietist position undoubtedly has contributed to the current state of political affairs in Muslim majority countries. Unfettered State power is and always will be expanding State power.

There was a third category of solutions they were exploring that Crone calls "anarchist." Most of these were what Crone calls "reluctant anarchists," in that they believed that the society could function without the Caliph. For them, anarchism was not an ideal they hoped to achieve, but the acknowledgment that the ideal, the Medina Caliphate, was lost, and could not be restored. They proposed a kind of evolutionary anarchism. They made no proposal to abolish private property, except to say that the illegitimacy of the ruler spoiled the validity of titles to property, presumably those granted by the ruler. This may be similar to the way some modern libertarians view eminent domain, corporate title, and intellectual property as invalid. Predominantly it was factions among the Mu'tazilites, the Kharijites, and the Sufis who proposed that if leaders kept turning into tyrants, perhaps they'd be better off without leaders at all.

Essentially they argued that the Caliph must be agreed upon by the entire community, either unanimously or by consensus, and that without this, no legitimate Caliph could exist. It was widely accepted that God did not impose obligations that were impossible to fulfill, so it was reasoned that there was no obligation to establish a legitimate Caliph, although hardly any of them denied the possibility of one emerging in the future. But in the meantime alternatives had to be explored. Some pointed out that the Bedouins had got along fine without rulers. Crone writes, "anarchists were clearly drawing on the tribal tradition which lies behind all early Islamic political thought of the type which may be loosely identified as libertarian."

Crone didn't specify this in the article, but this view of the Caliphate is consistent with the hadith in which the Prophet informed us that after him would be leaders who followed his example, then there would be kings, and then there would be tyrants. If you accept this hadith, it's clear that we have progressed from Caliphs to kings, and hard to argue we haven't progressed from kings to tyrants. Viewed this way, any attempt to reestablish the Caliphate by force could only result in further tyranny. Their specific reasons for arguing against the Caliphate is not particularly relevant to us today, as there has not been a Caliphate, legitimate of otherwise, since the collapse of the Ottoman Empire. The reality for us is that this is less an intellectual exercise than a practical necessity, especially in light of the tenuous grip the current tyrannies hold over their people.

Their proposed solutions of the "reluctant anarchists" ranged from a radical decentralization of public authority to a complete dissolution of public authority.

A subset of proposals involved replacing the Caliph with elected officials, the argument being that if you polled enough people, you minimized the danger of bias and collusion that had become the signature of the Caliphate. These proposals could be called "minarchist" in modern parlance. They proposed that people could elect trustworthy and learned leaders within their local communities, the argument being that there could never be unanimous agreement upon one leader of the Muslims, and one could not assess the quality of candidates at great distances. These leaders could either be completely independent of one another, or they could be joined together in a federation, the argument being that independent leaders would forever be fighting with their neighbors. This is strikingly reminiscent of the federalist vs. anti-federalist debate that took place in the American colonies 1,000 years later.

Some minarchists viewed these elected officials as temporary, only remaining in office when legal disputes arose, or when an enemy invaded. When the problem was resolved they would lose their positions, much as an imam does when he has finished leading prayer, and society could return to statelessness. This is very similar to the stateless judicial system in Somalia today, which we will discuss next.

Admittedly the minarchist proposals were not really anarchist. They advocated abolishing the form of government to which they had grown accustomed and replacing it with systems with far more public participation. Most of them were proposing new forms of government for which they had no historical precedent. But there were still some who were true anarchists in that they wanted a complete dissolution of public authority. Some argued that a sufficiently moral society would have no need for authority, while others argued that because society was not sufficiently moral, they couldn't have a legitimate authority. Either way, they believed that the welfare of society would be best if people were only left alone.

The most prominent group calling for the complete abolition of the State was a minority sect called the Najdiyya. They argued that so long as there was not sufficient agreement to establish a legitimate Caliph, there could never be enough to establish law at all. Even the consensus of scholars could not be a source of law in a community where no unified consensus existed anyway. To the Najdiyya every individual was responsible for his own salvation, and entitled to his own legal interpretations through independent reasoning (*ijtihad*). Indeed, any intellectual tradition must be built on this foundation, because in order to persuade others to adopt it, you must first appeal to their independent reasoning. The Najdiyya not only demanded political independence, but complete intellectual independence, because believers were, as the Prophet said, "like the teeth of a comb," and therefore should have no master but God Himself. Divine law could be conceived of as the natural law, available to all mankind, like fingerprints in the clay of Adam. Crone calls this "radical libertarianism," and as far as I can tell, it is one of the first appearances of it in history.

None of the anarchists or minarchists explained how to put their proposals into practice while the State still existed. They merely speculated, leaving it to future generations to implement their radical reform. We may be those generations. None of them proposed fomenting rebellion, happy to enjoy the comforts the State provided its intellectuals. Only the Sufis avoided material comforts, but their solution was simply to transcend politics and seek meaning in other pursuits, not to revolt.

However, in 817 anarchy was foisted upon them when the government in Baghdad collapsed. A civil war had ousted the previous Caliph and the influence of the new Caliph hadn't been established yet. Chaos ensued, and the public responded, as many would have predicted, by forming a vigilante group to protect private property, maintain commerce, and allow the meek to move freely through Baghdad. This is exactly the kind of spontaneous order we saw in

Egypt when police in plainclothes picked fights and looted stores. Civilians self-organized into neighborhood watch programs to protect each other. We see now what they saw then: in the absence of public authority there is a natural emergence of order out of chaos without central planning. The Muslim anarchists of the ninth century concluded, as many have in the modern world, "that when people are forced to rely on themselves, they discover talents they did not know they had."

# The Law According To The Somalis

Between earthquakes, droughts, and feuding warlords, the Muslim community is awash with relief efforts to benefit Somalia, as it should be. Somalia is pretty much the quintessential image of extreme poverty for most people. Nonetheless, sometimes a report appears that rightly points out that Somalia has improved by virtually every measure of standard of living since the collapse of their central government, and they've improved faster than any of their neighbors that still have a State. The percent of the population with access to medical facilities rose from 28% to 54.8%. Extreme poverty fell from 60% to 43.2%. Access to sanitation rose from 18% to 26%. The number of infants with low birth weight fell from 16 per thousand to 0.3, almost none. Even the BBC grudgingly admitted that "20 Years of Anarchy" had spurred economic growth, especially in the telecommunications sector.

*The Law of the Somalis* by Michael van Notten describes Somalia's stateless legal tradition, which he calls "kritarchy." It is perhaps the most groundbreaking, even moving piece I've read about justice in a stateless society. I am particularly interested in this topic because the majority of Somalia is Muslim, and as the rest of the Muslim world explodes into populist movements demanding Western democracy, I'd like to argue, as van Notten did, that a superior indigenous alternative is nestled right in their back yard.

Somalia is not stateless by accident, as is the conventional view. The Somali people consciously rejected democracy and central government, and with good reason. Prior to the colonial period, almost all African nations were polycentric tribal anarchies that practiced a system of customary law.

The Somalis never accepted the legal systems of the colonial powers, and largely ignored them or tried to nullify them by noncompliance, preferring always the social software of their own design. In 1991 the Republic of Somalia collapsed, but rather than electing a new leader, Somalis simply allowed their indigenous customary law to become the unopposed law of the land, which did not include any central government.

No discussion of Somalia can occur without addressing the political violence in and around the city of Mogadishu. So, why Mogadishu? Well, that's where the defunct politicians of the old republic, now known as "warlords," are attempting to reestablish a central government in the old capital.

The United States and the United Nations believe that a central government is necessary to bring Somalia into "the family of democratic nations," and they have spent billions of dollars on state-building efforts that only perpetuate the violence. Essentially, there is a huge pool of free money for whichever warlord can convincingly claim to be the central government of Somalia, but the people persistently resist all such claims. So warlords must use brute force, against both the people and each other, if they want the slush fund. Were it not for this, there would be little incentive for civil war.

Van Notten speculates that the reason the US and UN do this is ideological, and fundamentally rooted in their fear that if Somalia were allowed to succeed, its system of stateless law could be viewed as a viable alternative to democracy and be spread elsewhere.

Why are the Somali people consistently unimpressed with Western political systems?

To answer that, we've got to define four sources of law that Van Notten identifies in the book: natural law, contract law, statutory law, and customary law. Natural law is the voluntary primordial order of all human societies, which co-evolved with human nature. It is the invisible hand behind the entire human ecosystem. Natural law can be discovered and described, but it cannot be amended by human ambitions. A natural right is one that can be universalized to all human beings and exercised without permission and without infringing on the rights of others—namely, these are the rights to life, liberty, and property. Put simply, don't hurt people and don't take their stuff.

Contract law simply means to keep your agreements. A contract is valid when it is voluntarily entered into and does not violate the rights of any third party.

Statutory laws are those written by rulers and enforced through threats of violence, usually by a standing police force.

Customary law may be an unfamiliar concept, but once you learn to see it, you'll find it everywhere. Like natural law, it emerges spontaneously from people's voluntary interactions. Think of it like this: the laws of chemistry or physics are eternal, but the sciences of those disciplines are constantly evolving. Such is the relationship of natural law to customary law. Natural law is eternal, while customary law is the discipline of refining our understanding of it.

Natural law can only be pursued in ways consistent with itself, just as inconsistency disproves a law in science. In that sense, fraudulent contracts, barbaric customs, and oppressive statutes cannot be rightfully regarded as laws at all.

The Somalis are not ignorant of these concepts. In fact, life, liberty, property, and the four divisions of law all have words in their language that were not borrowed from other languages, indicating that these concepts are as indigenous to them as they are to English speakers. It was no historical accident that they developed a voluntary legal structure. Almost every Somali child is thoroughly educated in the customary law by the age of seven. Even an illiterate nomad understands life, liberty, and property, and regards himself as subject to no authority except God.

The Somali people strongly reject statutory systems like democracy because they render everyone subservient to political officials. They oppose dividing society into the rulers and the ruled. Democracy is often presented as "government by consent," but in any statutory regime, someone claims the authority to rule over those who don't consent. The inability to opt out by nonparticipation or secession renders the whole concept of consent meaningless. There can be no natural right to elect a "representative" to do what you have no natural right to do yourself. Further, the idea that rulers could write new laws would strike the Somali people as obscene, because in their view the law is preexistent.

They cherish natural rights like the right to self-defense by private arms, to practice law, to travel, to freely contract, to educate children, and to trade in open markets. In statutory systems, all of these are reduced to privileges requiring licenses. In natural law, one is free to engage in all of these activities without asking permission, and every license is an infringement on that right. In order to protect natural rights, statutory law must first violate natural rights; whereas customary law is designed to protect natural rights in ways that approximate natural law. In this sense, statutory democracy itself is incompatible with natural law.

So what is kritarchy? How does Somali customary law work?

The term "kritarchy" comes from the Greek terms *kritès* (judge) and *archè* (principle) and describes a social order where justice is the ruling principle. It's tempting to think of it as "rule by judges," but that's not really accurate. In a kritarchy, judges have no special powers and only hold their position by the consent of others. And there are no rules prohibiting anyone from serving as a judge. Disputing parties may choose anyone who has a good reputation, and it often happens that a clan has many judges. But a Somali judge only enforces the customary law, which is natural law as he understands it.

Traditional Somali society is decentralized, similar to the Internet. There is no executive or legislature. There is only a set of familiar protocols shared by a network of independent individuals organized into clans.

Now, you might think that a clan must have a chief who is the final arbiter in all matters. This is simply not the case. In fact, most Somali clans have origin stories about a distant past when their elders appointed a clan chief, but he was so oppressive or incompetent that they abolished the position and agreed never to appoint another.

Individuals are in no way obligated to their clan. Dissenters are never forced to participate in any clan activity, and individuals are free to leave their clan and either join another or form their own. There is no coercive hierarchy within the clan. Antisocial behavior only leads to social ostracism. If force must be used, it is never to destroy persons or property, but only to halt aggression.

The legal apparatus only comes into effect when there has been a violation of rights, as in personal injury or damage to property. All justice is restorative, not punitive. So if there is no victim, there is no crime. Somali law requires only that victims be compensated for violations of their life, liberty, and property.

A law court is formed when a conflict requires a third party to resolve it. If the disputants are from the same clan, they may go to the same judge, but if they are from different clans, judges from each family form a law court together. Judges are tasked with investigating the conflict and discovering a resolution that most satisfies the reason and conscience of both parties, not with rendering a verdict consistent with the precedents of other courts.

If the defendant is found to be at fault, compensation is owed to the victim for the damage caused. Somalis view humiliating or punishing a wrongdoer as a waste of time and resources, except that an additional fine may be awarded to the victim if the violation was intentional. The task of deterrence or rehabilitation is left to the clan of the wrongdoer, because they are ultimately liable for him.

So in the case of injury, the wrongdoer may be obliged to provide medical care as the victim recovers. In the case of theft, the stolen property must be returned and the victim compensated for their trouble. In the case of property damage, the property must be repaired or replaced. Although it is rare, in the case of homicide a murderer may be executed, but more often the bereaved family will agree to compensation, which is called the "blood price." It is always up to the victim, not the judge, to decide to what extent to enforce the verdict.

All cases are widely discussed in the community, and if there is a consensus that the judge is not performing to the people's satisfaction, he may lose the confidence of his clan, and will likely not be asked to settle future conflicts. In this way, judges are always subject to open competition.

Should enforcement be necessary within one clan, the court may request that able-bodied men in the community volunteer as a temporary police force, but there are no standing police. They may only use the minimum force necessary to right what was wronged. However, if the conflict was between multiple clans, one clan has no power to enforce its verdict on another. Penalties can be imposed for refusing to comply with a verdict, but clans are expected to police their own, and there are mechanisms in place to incentivize this.

Every clan maintains a communal fund that members voluntarily contribute to. This fund operates as a kind of social insurance for every Somali against liability. It can be used both to provide welfare for clan members who fall on hard times and as venture capital for businessmen to borrow and invest. If a person owes restitution that they cannot afford to pay, they must approach their clan to have their liability covered by this insurance fund.

This can be painfully embarrassing, and it gives the clan an opportunity to chastise the person, but it also ensures that victims can always be made whole. In the case of conflict between multiple clans, this allows the clan of the victim to seek restitution from the insurance fund of the clan of the wrongdoer, which incentivizes clans to police their own. If habitual violators of the law become a drain on the clan's insurance fund, they may have their membership terminated, making them outlaws with no protection from any court.

In principle, this description of the kritarchy in Somalia will seem very familiar to any student of natural law. However, in practice some of the customs which have evolved are so specific to their cultural and historical context that they seem utterly foreign.

Some customs are also stifling to economic development, which may explain why growth has been slower than we might predict in a stateless society. For example, customary law has been very reluctant to extend property rights to land. Instead land is owned by the clan, and an elaborate system of land-use customs have developed. This makes a kind of sense for a nomadic pastoral society, but for the development of modern infrastructure, land ownership is key.

In addition, foreigners have no protection in the Somali legal system (unless they are accepted by a host clan), and they are completely prohibited from owning land. The logic behind this is that they are not insured against liability the way clan members are; but discouraging foreign trade has stifled both economic growth and cultural cross-pollination.

Other customs are utterly barbaric by modern standards. Some clans use very primitive physical punishment for delinquent youth, as in tying them to a tree covered with honey and allowing them to be bitten by ants. The worst practices described in the book are those impacting women. In one case a verdict against a rapist obliged him to marry the woman he raped, the logic being that the damage he'd caused her was to spoil her marriageability. Some of these customs are so incredibly backward that they can only be understood with the detachment of an anthropologist, which van Notten provides.

Obviously, these customs have no place in natural law. It is incredibly important to understand that Somalia's customary law is not being presented as a panacea, but that the elegant legal structure of kritarchy and its potential compatibility with natural law is a superior foundation for future development than is democracy.

To understand this point, imagine for a moment that customs like these were enshrined in the statutes of a democratic system. History shows us that social change precedes political change, and forcing the political apparatus to reflect social change is a slow process requiring mass movements, civil disobedience, and even civil war.

Customary law, on the other hand, evolves literally simultaneously with social change. It consists of the rules that judges discern from the normative behavior of living people. If social change occurs gradually, custom will change gradually; and if social change occurs suddenly, custom will change suddenly—because custom is changed by voluntary acceptance, not by democratic process.

Kritarchy can only exist in societies where the custom of seeking justice is stronger than the custom of achieving political goals through coercion. For democracy the opposite is true. For that reason, kritarchy is eminently suited to protect natural rights.

Kritarchy in Somalia challenges the conventional view that tribal societies had no concept of property and contract, because even without a central government Somalia has since time immemorial engaged in free trade, where prices are determined by market forces, and competition prevented the emergence of monopolies.

The Somalis have demonstrated that providing justice in the free market is at least possible, and that you don't need to pass statutes prohibiting murder and theft, because those laws already exist, whether you write them down or not. In short, they have demonstrated that life, liberty, and property are inscribed upon the hearts of mankind, like fingerprints in the clay of Adam.

# Chapter Two: Fiat Money

## The Dust of Riba and the Rush for Gold

"There will come a time when you will not be able to find a single person in the world who will not be consuming riba. And if anyone claims that he is not consuming riba then surely the dust of riba will reach him." — Abu-Dawood Hadith 3325—Narrated by Ibn Isa

The Messenger of Allah is reported to have said, "A time is certainly coming over mankind in which there will be nothing left that will be of use save a Dinar and a Dirham"—Musnad, Ahmad ibn Hanbal—Narrated by Abu Bakr ibn Abi Maryam.

The Arabic word *riba* literally means "increase." Generally we understand it to mean "usury" or "interest." In exchange for the privilege of a loan, the borrower pays the lender an additional percentage of the loan's sum. Sharia defines numerous other forms of riba, but this is the most common form in the modern world. Historically money lending of this type was forbidden in all prophetic traditions.

The earliest prohibitions of usury come from 4,000-year-old Vedic texts, the oldest religious manuscripts of Hinduism. In the Jatakas Tales of Buddhism, roughly 2,500 years old, usurious lenders are referred to as "hypocritical ascetics" (1). The Torah refers to usury as *neshekh*, meaning "a bite" and *avak ribbit*, literally "the dust of interest" (1). Sound familiar? Numerous warnings throughout the Bible guided Jews and Christians of the past to acknowledge the inherent injustice of such transactions. Deuteronomy 23:20 reads, "You shall not demand interest from your countrymen on a loan of money or of food or of anything else on which interest is usually demanded." In the middle ages the Catholic Church interpreted passages like this as a strict prohibition against charging interest on a loan. It was the teaching of Thomas Aquinas that the purpose of money was to serve the greater good of the people by facilitating the exchange of goods needed to live a pious life. Adherents of all these faiths once recognized that such an economic system funneled wealth out of the hands of the borrowing class, into the hands of the lending class, further separating the rich and poor. In the modern world it is Muslim scholars who preach the dangers of interest. Just as Thomas Aquinas, and Aristotle before him, they teach the inherent oppression of usurious transactions, and they teach the use of money to promote the general welfare, to establish economic justice, and to serve as a medium of voluntary exchange and charity.

So... what is money? If you search Google for a definition of "dollar," the first result will be "the basic monetary unit equal to 100 cents." Which begs the question: What is a cent? To that, you'll receive the result: "a fractional monetary unit worth one-hundredth of the value of the basic unit." It's circular!

The monetary system in the United States is built upon a hidden usury known as inflation. In 1913 the US Congress passed the Federal Reserve Act granting monopoly power to print money to the Federal Reserve System. The concept of the Federal Reserve System was actually not devised by the US Congress, but by a group of international bankers who met in secret on an island off the coast of Georgia (2). The first fraud perpetuated by this system is the name itself. The Federal Reserve System is not federal. It's owned by private shareholders, motivated by private profits. The Federal Reserve System is not a reserve. There is no gold. There is no silver. They print a baseless paper note. Its only value is derived from public confidence in its stability... which is declining. The Federal Reserve System is not a system. At the time, "system" was understood to mean that it was a decentralized network of banks, but it is really a central bank with many branches. Central banking was bitterly opposed by the drafters of the Constitution. The founders recognized the importance of honest currency, and they understood inflation, which is why they wrote in the Constitution, "No State shall... make any Thing but gold and silver Coin a Tender in Payment of Debts."(3)

So, why perpetuate this fraud? How does Congress benefit? The answer is near limitless credit. The Federal Reserve gives Congress the ability to borrow money to fund their projects without directly taxing their subjects. But where does the money come from? It simply springs into being the moment they sign the loan. Unable to fund its devastatingly expensive wars throughout the world, the US government has abandoned the stability of a gold standard and embraced a fraudulent system of fiat currency. Fiat currency is paper printed by The Fed and borrowed by the government. The dollar is not backed by any commodity. It derives its value from legal tender laws that obligate subjects to use the dollar. Ironically, the dollar also behaves like a commodity in the market, and like all commodities, it becomes subject to the market pressures of supply and demand.

Here's the dust:

When the government borrows money from the Fed (with interest, of course) they circulate an ever-increasing amount of paper notes into the economy. Increased supply means decreased demand. The more they print, the less value the money already in the system holds. This is the cause of inflation. Most people incorrectly believe that inflation is the rising cost of products, but this is only the result. Inflation is actually the increases in the money supply that lower the buying power of the dollar. When the Fed prints money to pay for the government's war spending, the buying power of that new money is stolen from the buying power of the dollar in your pocket. It's an invisible interest that is built into the US monetary system. The Fed then obfuscates this by manipulating the interest rates on loans and savings accounts. So, while the dollar amount in a savings account may increase by interest, the actual value is decreased by inflation. Since the inception of the Fed, the buying power of the US dollar has dropped 97%. So today's dollar is worth only 3 cents compared to the gold dollar of 1913. Soon it will not be worth the paper it's printed on, and this country will enter into the same economic recession that toppled the Soviet Union. Fiat currency is a fraud. Like all forms of usury, it funnels money out of the hands of the borrower—the government, and, by proxy, the American people—and into the hands of the lender: the Fed, and therefore the international bankers.

The Prophet Muhammad (peace be upon him) predicted this economic catastrophe when he said that one of the signs of the approach of the Hour is that wealth will increase to such an extent that one will not be satisfied if given one hundred dinars (4). Sharia defines a dinar as 4.25 grams of 22k gold. At the time of writing this the price of gold just passed $1,000 per ounce. That's a value of about $136. One hundred gold dinars at that price would hold the purchasing power of about $13,600 (425g of gold). Let's compare that with the purchasing power of the dinar in the time of the Prophet. One Hadith describes the Prophet purchasing an old camel for 4 dinars (5). In US dollars that's $544. Another Hadith describes a gold and pearl necklace purchased for 7 or 9 dinars (6). In today's market that's $952 or $1,224. A similar Hadith is narrated of a gold necklace studded with gems being sold for 12 dinars (7), which is $1,632. These are not unreasonable prices in today's market. The purchasing power of gold has remained relatively stable for 1,400 years, and throughout history. It's the value of the dollar, and fiat currencies like it, that fluctuate and decline. Today most Muslim-majority countries have abandoned the gold dinar and instead based their currency on the US dollar. Today 100 Kuwaiti dinars hold the purchasing power of $366 (11.4g of gold). 100 Libyan dinars hold the purchasing power of $84 (2.6g of gold). 100 Iraqi dinars hold the purchasing power of just 8 cents (.002g of gold)(8). If you take this Hadith to mean 100 gold dinars, the value has not changed. 425 grams of 22k gold is still 425 grams of 22k gold. But if you take it to mean 100 of the fiat dinars printed in any Muslim majority country, it has already come to pass. So, while the Kuwaiti dinar can boast that it is the highest valued monetary unit in the world

(9), it is worth only 3% of the value of the gold dinar prescribed by Sharia. This is because printing fiat money debases a currency, harms an economy, funnels wealth into the hands of the lenders, and levies an invisible usury against the poor.

The solution to this looming economic crisis is obvious: return to the Sunnah. Invest in gold and silver. Exchange in gold and silver. This is surprisingly easier than it sounds. Since 1992, e-dinar.com has minted gold dinars and silver dirhams in the traditional denominations. In 2000 they launched a digital gold system that can be transferred like PayPal. So far, few Muslims have taken an interest in Sunnah money in the US, but gold is becoming increasingly more accessible in US markets through companies like Midas Resources. The Free Lakota Bank, of the Lakota Nation issues and circulates a silver currency. In New Hampshire, Shire Silver facilitates using precious metals in trade by measuring, certifying, and packaging small bullion bars in denominations suitable for exchange.

Imagine this scenario: Say you own a grocery and a customer comes in to purchase a loaf of bread costing $1.50. In exchange he offers you a choice: You can either accept six quarters, composed of 92% copper and 8% nickel, or one silver dirham of equal value, composed of pure silver. Which would you take? The wise grocer would take the silver, and here's why: If you hold the six quarters and the one dirham in a safe for thirty years, the dirham will still buy a loaf of bread, and the quarters will likely not buy a slice of bread. Precious metals are inflation-proof because they hold intrinsic value. Their value may fluctuate with the market, but they cannot be devalued by the actions of Congress and the Fed. If that's not enough of an incentive, consider this: If you take the quarters, you have made a sale, on which the government collects a sales tax from the buyer and an income tax on the seller; if you take the dirham, you have not made a sale—you've traded two commodities of equal value, with no US dollars exchanged. Using gold and silver as a medium of exchange keeps a community's wealth in the community. Imagine the baraka in conducting your transactions, paying your zakat and sadaqa, or even giving a marriage gift in the denominations of the Sunnah.

The first and most important step is something you can do right where you're sitting now: Make the intention. In your heart, believe that gold and silver are real money, and that fiat money is a usurious fraud. The next step is to educate yourself and other Muslims around you about these important subjects. Share this information with others. Copy it and distribute it. Locate and read The Gold Dinar and Silver Dirham: Islam and the Future of Money by Imran N. Hosein (10). Copy it and distribute it. It's time that Muslims took steps toward protecting economic justice, both for themselves, and the society they live in. A basic economic principle is that good money exposes bad money. It's time to revive this long-lost Sunnah.


For more info:

(1) *History of Usury Prohibition* by Wayne A. M. Visser and Alastair McIntosh
(2) *The Creature From Jekyll Island* by G. Edward Griffin
(3) US Constitution: Article I, Section 10, Paragraph 1, Clause 5
(4) Bukhari, Volume 4, Book 53, Number 401
(5) Bukhari, Volume 3, Book 38, Number 504
(6) Abu-Dawood Book 22, Number 3345
(7) Sahih Muslim Book 010, Number 386
(8) http://www.oanda.com
(9) http://en.wikipedia.org/wiki/Kuwaiti_dinar
(10) www.imranhosein.org

# China Is Plotting Against the Dollar Hegemony

When people think about inflation—increases in the money supply—they usually imagine that some group of career economists at the Fed and Treasury are churning numbers to determine just how much they can debase the currency without completely collapsing the economy. Even as they acknowledge that the monetary system is flawed, and the value of the dollar will continue to tank, they take some comfort in believing that some bureaucrat someplace is in control of the situation and can at least ensure some predictability in the rate of inflation.

What these people may not realize is that printing money is not the only way to increase the money supply. In fact, a great deal of money already in existence is not currently reflected in the domestic economy because it is being held in reserve in foreign countries. If those countries ever decide to spend those dollars by exchanging them for some other reserve, those dollars will come back into the domestic economy, resulting in the same price inflation caused by printing money—only this time, no trusty American bureaucrat has a hand on the brakes. If a global economy's worth of dollars ever floods back into the domestic economy, you'll see hyperinflation to the point that burning money will be a more efficient source of heat than buying firewood.

WikiLeaks released a 2009 US State Department internal cable from the Embassy in Beijing that illustrates my point perfectly. The cable describes China's plan to undermine the US dollar hegemony by increasing China's gold reserves.

From 2003 to 2008 China increased their gold reserves from 600 tonnes to 1054 tonnes by converting roughly $11 billion of US dollar reserves to gold. The average price of gold during that five-year period was $677/ounce. Renowned gold forecaster Julian D. W. Phillips has predicted that China intends to increase its reserves to 5000 tonnes by 2013. If gold stays the price it is today (Yeah, right!), which is $1800/ounce, that's roughly $250 billion of US dollar reserves.

According to the leaked cable, this increase in China's gold reserves is intended to "kill two birds with one stone." First, it serves as a model for other countries to encourage reserving more gold, and therefore fewer US dollars. Second, it strengthens the Chinese currency, the renminbi, so that it can begin to replace the declining US dollar as the world reserve currency. All of this spells bad news for the American economy.

The leaked cable also reveals something interesting about the price of gold in international markets. It reads, "The US and Europe have always suppressed the rising price of gold. They intend to weaken gold's function as an international reserve currency... Suppressing the price of gold is very beneficial for the US in maintaining the US dollar's role as the international reserve currency."

The Gold Anti-Trust Action Committee (GATA) has asserted for over a decade that the quantity of gold held by the world's central banks was over-reported to keep the price of gold artificially low. GATA's research indicates that there is a gold cartel by which the US government suppresses the market price of gold through various intermediaries like Goldman Sachs and JPMorgan Chase.

The price of gold is a barometer, a canary in a coal mine, of global market health. In a free market, gold prices should move inversely to interest rates and the value of government bonds. In other words, you can't control interest rates, and can't sustain a fiat currency long term if you don't prevent a real free market in precious metals. Ironically, suppressing the price of gold may simply be making it that much cheaper for foreign countries to dump their US dollars.

# Barter with Silver Is "Domestic Terrorism"

In a landmark case against the Liberty Dollar, a privately minted silver medallion, US Attorney Anne Tompkins stated, "Attempts to undermine the legitimate currency of this country are simply a unique form of domestic terrorism." The quote was repeated in the press release of the FBI's Charlotte, North Carolina, office.

This of course presumes that the US dollar, the Federal Reserve Note, is a legitimate currency. In fact, the government's current monetary policy is in violation of its Constitutional mandate, which promises, "No State shall... make any Thing but gold and silver Coin a Tender in Payment of Debts." (Article I, Section 10)

After an eight-day trial, and less than two hours of jury deliberation, the monetary architect of the Liberty Dollar, Bernard von NotHaus, was convicted on multiple counterfeiting-related charges, including making coins similar to US coins, issuing, passing, selling, and possessing said coins, intending to use said coins as "current money," and conspiracy against the United States. He is facing 25 years in prison, $750,000 in fines, and the forfeiture of over 16,000 pounds of precious metal, an estimated $7 million value when it was seized in 2007.

Apparently I'm not a Muslim terrorist, just a terrorist who happens to be Muslim. Longtime readers know that I am a strong advocate of honest currency. What they may not know is that I too have passed, sold, and possessed Liberty Dollars. So, according to the US attorney in this case, I too am guilty of "domestic terrorism." Yet, I don't feel guilty, for some reason.

After ten years of legitimate business, there were an estimated $20 million in Liberty Dollars in circulation. Then on November 14th, 2007, the headquarters and mint of the Liberty Dollar was raided by the FBI, who seized everything: the computers, the records, the money, the silver, the gold—everything. What the Feds perhaps did not consider is that the precious metals they seized were not the property of Liberty Dollar, but the property of hundreds of thousands of private individuals, myself included. I have in my possession a silver certificate bearing a serial number corresponding to a measure of silver that was being housed there and has now been seized by the FBI. A class action lawsuit was filed by thousands of people for the return of our stolen property.

The prosecution argued that because the silver medallions were marked with a manufacturer's suggested retail value in dollars, the word "USA," the Statue of Liberty, and other common iconography on US currency, they could be mistaken for legal tender—even though they don't look like any official coin, primarily because they are actually made of silver, not zinc and tin foil, but also because there is a website and 800 number printed right on the face of the coin. Not to mention that the lot that was seized in the raid bore the likeness of Congressman Ron Paul, another strong advocate of honest currency. Last I checked, no US coin had Ron Paul's face on it.

In fact, all Liberty Dollar marketing collateral explicitly states that they are non-government currency, intended as an inflation-proof alternative to the baseless Federal Reserve Note. At their inception NotHaus stated, "We're going to be to the Federal Reserve System what Federal Express was to the Post Office." The prosecution even admitted in trial that the silver medallions were of full weight and purity, and sold as advertised, which is why no fraud charges were made. We're not talking about counterfeiting. Counterfeiting without fraud is nonsense. We're talking about competition.

Tompkins went on to say that NotHaus's activities, "do not involve violence," but that they "represent a clear and present danger to the economic stability of this country." Can you imagine? If private individuals bartering with measures of silver is a danger to the economic stability of this country, that should tell you just how bankrupt the dollar is. NotHaus faces what is essentially a life sentence in prison, the seizure of all his assets, and the destruction of his life's work because the federal government is terrified that you will wake up to this scam. NotHaus did not force anyone to accept his coins. He did not lie to anyone about what he was selling. All he did was recognize that there was a demand in the market from consumers like me to trade in currency that could not be deliberately inflated by the government.

Tompkins concludes by saying, "We are determined to meet these threats through infiltration, disruption, and dismantling of organizations which seek to challenge the legitimacy of our democratic form of government." To whatever extent NotHaus intended to challenge the legitimacy of US monetary policy, he should be completely protected under the First Amendment.

If we are not free to exchange goods and services for gold and silver in private transactions, nor free even to advocate for the repeal of the Federal Reserve Act, then indeed US currency is backed by bullets.

# Gadaffi's Gold

Despite numerous assurances from our fearless Executioner in Chief that American boots would not trample the sands of Libya, that's exactly what happened. Best of all, Obama sought NATO approval instead of Congressional approval, as his Constitutional mandate prescribes. But don't worry—Pentagon spokesman Captain John Kirby assured us these troops were only expected to be there for a short while. Days, not weeks. Or was it months, not years? Whichever.

The question is, why Libya? They claimed it was about protecting civilians, but if America is really in the business of liberating people from tyrants, wouldn't it make more sense to intervene in Syria, or, for God's sake, Saudi Arabia? The postcards from the Saudi Ministry of Tourism would probably make good fund-raising material for Human Rights Watch.

So, it must be oil, right? Well... Canada and Mexico both individually produce more barrels than Libya. And again, Saudi Arabia produces more than all of those countries combined. So, what gives? Like so many things in this world, the motivation of those plotting in their smoky rooms probably has more to do with the currency than anything else

Think of the US dollar as a Ponzi scheme that requires an ever-increasing pool of gullible dupes to keep the scam going. The Federal Reserve has already inflated the money supply far beyond what the domestic economy can absorb, so they must seek more dupes overseas. In 1971 the US made a deal to keep the Saudis in power if they agreed to only trade oil in dollars. This ensured a whole global market full of dupes who would have to use US dollars if they wanted to trade with the largest oil producer in the world. That is why the US dollar has been the reserve currency of the world, and why Saudi Arabia enjoys such a privileged status in American politics.

Do you see? America's foreign policy is not about importing oil. It's about exporting US dollars. To keep the Ponzi scheme going, they must ensure that the rest of the world continues to use US dollars to buy and sell oil. There's just one problem: If the world ever wakes up, it means the end of dollar hegemony, and the most devastating economic collapse in history. So, those who threaten to wake up the world must be dealt with.

This is why the US props up some tyrants and takes out others, and why they attack some oil-rich nations and defend others. Just six months before the US invaded Iraq, Saddam Hussein announced they would be pricing Iraqi oil in Euros instead of US dollars.

Whatever weapons he was hiding and atrocities he was committing didn't matter to US policy-makers. It was the monetary change that triggered the invasion.

Now US intervention in Libya makes sense.

Gaddafi imagined Libya as some kind of socialist paradise and himself as the self-proclaimed "Brotherly Leader and Guide of the Revolution." Anyone who has flipped through Gaddafi's "Little Green Book" has to wonder if he wasn't putting LSD in his Nescafé. His economic acumen was not exactly well-developed, but one area where he was uncharacteristically lucid is monetary policy.

Under Gaddafi, the Central Bank of Libya was completely state-run, funded by the country's vast oil wealth. It issued interest-free loans, and its own currency, the Libyan dinar, which was not controlled by international banks. So, in order to do business in Libya, other nations had to go through the Libyan Central Bank. Gaddafi's plan was to quit selling Libyan oil in US dollars, and to make matters worse for the Fiat Empire, he was preparing to demand gold as payment.

In both 1996 and 2000, Gaddafi organized the World Mathaba Conference, where he called on Arab and African nations to refuse the US dollar and the Euro, and adopt a new international currency. Before the US intervention in Libya, Gaddafi was on the verge of launching the Islamic Gold Dinar.

The gold dinar would have transformed Libya into an economic powerhouse in the region. At the time, Libya held an estimated 144 tons of gold. American press was almost completely silent about Gaddafi's gold dinar, but *Russia Today*, Al Jazeera, and the international press reported this as the reason for US intervention almost exclusively. Experts said the move had the potential to wreak havoc on the US economy as all those dollars flooded back to US shores. You see, gold and silver currency is the single greatest threat to the dollar's hegemony.

Adding weight to the theory, the first thing the Rebels did upon taking control of Benghazi was create a central bank and paper currency to replace Gaddafi's state-run monetary system. This occurred while they were still in the midst of their struggle for independence, before they even had a government. The decision was broadcast to the world in the early weeks of the conflict, and even though American media was silent about it, you can bet American policy-makers got the message. Robert Wenzel wrote in the *Economic Policy Journal*: "I have never before heard of a central bank being created in just a matter of weeks out of a popular uprising. This suggests we have a bit more than a rag tag bunch of rebels running around and that there are some pretty sophisticated influences."

If I had to guess, I'd say those "sophisticated influences" were power brokers determined to quash the gold dinar, not to liberate the

Libyan people. It's pretty simple, really: International banks fund the rebellion through the central bank. The Rebels offer their nation's resources as collateral on the loan. When the Rebels can't make the interest payments, Libya becomes another in a long list of nations enslaved by debt to multinational corporations.

So, knowing this, what is the US's next target?

Iran has priced oil in US dollars since a treaty they signed after World War II, but like Libya, it is one of a short list of nations that has an independent state-run central bank. Well, now Iran is dumping its US dollar reserves in trade with Russia, China, and Japan, and whisperings are beginning to surface that in the very near future, none of Iran's oil will be traded in dollars. US officials have stated explicitly that weakening the Central Bank is a primary goal of US sanctions against Iran. Are you seeing a pattern developing? If a foreign power doesn't bow to the dollar hegemony, first they can expect sanctions, then "regime change" —just like Libya, just like Iraq.

US wars are not about terrorism, or democracy, or even really about oil. They are about forcing the world to accept the supremacy of the dollar in international markets, because even though the dollar isn't backed by gold or silver, it's clearly backed by lead and depleted uranium.

# The Malaysian Liberty Dollar

Harsh criticisms of Islam and Muslims are increasingly common in Western media, but one area where they continue to command respect is in the financial sector, especially among Austrian economists. In the wake of a mortgage meltdown, a recession, and unprecedented national debt, many have observed that Islamic finance, specifically its prohibition on interest, has shielded many Muslims from economic crisis.

Kelantan, a state within the nation of Malaysia, took it one step further by issuing a currency that would protect consumers from the problem of inflation and market manipulation inherent to any debt-based paper currency. The Islamic Party of Malaysia, currently the ruling party of Kelantan, believes the solution comes from Islamic history, when the dinar and the dirham were gold and silver coins.

In August 2010 the Islamic Party of Malaysia announced the launch of a gold dinar and silver dirham intended as an alternative to the Malaysian ringgit in the state of Kelantan. Over 1,000 stores agreed to accept the coins, and Perak announced that it would be the second Malaysian state to use the alternative currency.

In 2002 Malaysian Prime Minister Mahathir Mohamed began advocating using the Islamic Gold Dinar (IGD) in international trade between Muslim central banks, but the Kelantan dinar is no international currency. It's intended for use in private transaction in the open market.

The Malaysian federal government opposed the move, arguing that only the central bank, Bank Negara Malaysia, has the authority to issue currency. But who can blame them? They were probably just trying to avoid Gaddafi's fate. The Malaysian International Trade and Industry Minister Datuk Seri Mustapa Mohamed said, "I advise the Kelantan government not to do so [issue currency] as it likes. Matters concerning currency comes under the jurisdiction of the federal government, and not the state government, and what had been done clearly breached the country's law."

But what if the currency wasn't issued by any state? What if it was a product of the free market?

MyNET Capital, an online precious metal trader in Kuala Lumpur, seized upon this opportunity to launch the "One World 10 Dirham" to be sold across twenty-five countries including Malaysia. At the time some called it "The Malaysian Liberty Dollar." The silver dirham was chosen over the gold dinar because, as MyNET executive chairman Terry Ghani said, "It's a tactical asset because you can capitalize on price appreciation... at the same time a strategic asset as a long-term wealth preservation." Silver coins are more affordable for middle-income consumers because they can be bought in small amounts and according to the customer's capacity. They are more mobile than real estate and less volatile than stocks and other commodities, making them an effective long-term hedge against inflation.

The 10-dirham coin is 29.75g of pure silver, just a hair under a troy ounce. The obverse of the coin shows an intricate piece of Arabic calligraphy that reads "Salamu Alaikum," meaning "Peace Be Upon You." An interlinking geometric design is intended to convey a message of universal peace and harmony between all the diverse peoples of the world. The reverse is in English and reads "1 WORLD — May Peace Be Upon Our Planet," and below it, "To Create, To Preserve, and To Prosper." Ghani said, "This is the world's first dirham inscribed in English to propagate its knowledge and appreciation amongst the global non-Arab-speaking community."

Advocates of the gold and silver currency argue that precious metals are the only honest measure of value, and that paper currency is a kind of fraud or usury. When a currency has no commodity backing it, there is no limit on the amount a central bank can increase the money supply, and therefore no limit on inflation. The result is that the buying power of the new money is taken away from the buying power of the money already in circulation, which leads to rising prices.

So I wonder—if the US will violently topple foreign leaders like Gaddafi to protect the US Dollar hegemony, and we've seen the government attack domestic free market silver currencies like the Liberty Dollar, how will the US attack foreign free market silver currencies like the One World 10 Dirham?

# US Dollar vs. Monopoly Money

Economists use a lot of illustrative examples of hyperinflation in history. You'll hear about wheelbarrows full of cash buying a loaf of bread, or pension checks only buying one cup of coffee. Or they'll tell you about store owners doubling their prices day to day, or governments simply stamping old bills with extra zeros just to keep up. These examples all seem distant and foreign, fundamentally implausible to most Americans. But I think I've found an example that really drives the concept home.

The board game Monopoly from Parker Brothers is for many a quintessential symbol of capitalism. So much so that the game's mascot, Rich Uncle Pennybags, is a frequent character in socialist political cartoons.

The first edition of Monopoly was made by Hasbro in 1935 and sold for just $2. Each set contained 15,140 Monopoly Dollars (MP$). So, in 1935 the exchange rate of MP$ to US Dollars was 1/7,570. In other words a US Dollar cost 7,570 MP$.

If you walk into a toy store today, behind all the special editions, the retail price on the standard Monopoly is about $12. Measured this way, the US Dollar costs 1,261.66 MP$. That's an 84% drop. Not bad, but you have to keep in mind that the 1935 edition came with wood and metal pieces, complete with wooden carrying case. So it's not a fair comparison.

In 1985, Parker Brothers released a 50th Anniversary Commemorative edition that was made with the original materials. The set contained the same 15,140 MP$ with a retail value of $40. So, in 1985 the US Dollar cost 378.5 MP$. A 95% drop. In 2002 they produced another replica of the original 1935 set. It sold for $80, reducing the cost of the US Dollar to 189.25 MP$. By the time the 75th Anniversary rolled around, they'd stopped making them out of wood. Instead they launched the 2010 Monopoly Revolution edition, which was still made of plastic and cardboard... but this time it was a circle instead of a square! Such is inflation. This is the board game equivalent of minting a new dollar coin made out of copper and pot metal, brushing it with brass and calling it a "golden dollar." Or printing new bills with flashy new colored ink to distract people from the fact that the original materials are no longer affordable.

Let's put this in perspective. In the 67 years from 1935 to 2002 the price of the US Dollar in Monopoly money went from 7,570 MP$ to 189.25 MP$. That's a 97.5% reduction in the value of the US Dollar... measured against *Monopoly money*!

I'm not sure how to make it any clearer: Uncle Pennybags has a better monetary policy than Uncle Sam. Someday economists may warn future generations about hyperinflation with examples of Americans preferring to buy Park Place with cash.

# Chapter Three: Terrorism

## Why "They" Hate "Us"

After 9/11 many Americans were utterly baffled why America had been attacked. The average American had never considered how their government's foreign policy affected the outside world. Hanging heavy in the minds of every American was the question, "Why do they hate us?"

President Bush offered a simple, yet insufficient explanation: "They hate our freedoms." This would make sense if they had first attacked Switzerland, Canada, or any of the other nations that score higher than the US on the State of World Liberty Index. But analysts who offered more in-depth answers were decried as blaming America, or sympathizing with the enemy.

To answer this question we need another approach. The Information Clearing House published a chronology of US intervention in the Middle East beginning in the 1920s. So, what happens if we reverse the roles? In this thought experiment East becomes West, Muslim becomes Christian, and oil will become unobtainium, the fictional mineral from the movie *Avatar*.

This can't be a perfect analogy of real history, and it certainly isn't meant to attribute blame, or justify violence. It is only an attempt to understand the emotions of those who hate America. While reading, I encourage you to try not to imagine real history, but instead just remain aware of how you feel.

### 1930s
*Economic control over the United States*
Huge deposits of unobtainium are discovered in the United States. The Ottoman Empire (OE) pressures American energy corporations to form a cartel that grants them the exclusive privilege to mine the unobtainium. The OE profits in billions of dollars from the refinement and sale of American unobtainium while the United States is weakened by two world wars. During negotiations over the unobtainium resources, the Ottoman Sultan drafts a map dividing American mines between Turkish, Arabian, and Persian corporations. In the process the American Union is broken into separate client states, and the OE emerges as the dominant power in the world.

### 1940s
*A sovereign Native American State*

The OE pushes a resolution through the United Nations converting most of New Jersey into the Pan-Indian state of Turtle Island. New York City is divided into East New York, which remains American, and West New York, which becomes Turtle Island's capital. Liberty Island, home of the Statue of Liberty, becomes a pilgrimage site for Native Americans.

War erupts between Turtle Island and New York, Pennsylvania, Connecticut, and Delaware. Two-thirds of the American population of New Jersey is forced to flee to surrounding states.

### 1950s
#### Upheaval of the American States
The MAH, the central intelligence agency of the OE, instigates a military coup to overthrow the elected government of Texas and installs an Emperor who rules by torturing, killing, and imprisoning his political opponents.

The democratic governments of multiple American states are overthrown by MAH-financed coups and replaced with military dictatorships. When revolutionary rebellion breaks out, the OE dispatches thousands of troops to preserve stability and prepare for possible future intervention. The OE also heavily arms some American states, encouraging them to conscript American troops to prevent other American states from attempting to reestablish an American Union. The MAH attempts to assassinate the governor of New York, who is the strongest proponent of a new American Union.

The Ottoman Sultan threatens to detonate a nuclear weapon on American soil if any American state resists his military presence.

### 1960s
#### The Socialist coup of California
The OE works to undermine the California government by supporting Mexican separatists, and supporting a coup by the Ottoman-backed Socialist Party. This campaign includes public executions of thousands of the California Socialist Party's political opponents.

The OE then stands by while the new Socialist Party kills many of the Mexican separatists they once supported.

### 1970s
#### The Texan Revolution
Armed by the OE, Turtle Island seizes the rest of New Jersey, along with parts of Delaware and the rest of New York City. Thousands are killed with napalm. The Ottoman Sultan again threatens a nuclear attack if the Soviet Union intervenes on America's behalf.

A revolution to unseat the Emperor begins in Texas. Hundreds of Texans are burned to death, and 10,000 are massacred at the state capital. The Emperor is forced to flee and receives protection in the OE, despite demands that he be returned to face trial.

California invades Texas with OE support. But the OE also secretly supports Texas by supplying them with weapons. Prolonging the war weakens both sides and solidifies OE control over both. Over a million die on both sides.

### 1980s
*The Soviet invasion of Alaska*

The OE increases its military presence in the Bible Belt, and the Soviet Union increases its military presence in Texas as they compete for control of the unobtainium supply. The OE begins supplying Christian fundamentalists with weapons to fight the Soviets in Alaska, which the OE considers a buffer state.

Armed with OE weapons, Turtle Island invades Connecticut, killing thousands, assassinating the governor, and massacring over 1,000 unarmed women and children.

By the time Soviet troops withdraw from Alaska, over a million Alaskans are dead, and one-third of the population is living in refugee camps.

### 1990s
*The OE invasion of California*

The dictator the OE originally backed in California against Texas launches a poison-gas attack on California's Mexican separatists. He then attempts to invade Oregon. So, the OE invades, systematically destroying California's electrical and water systems, and killing 200,000 civilians in 100 hours.

After the assault, the OE imposes trade sanctions against California, blocking humanitarian and medical aid. About a million civilians die from disease and malnutrition, including 300,000 children.

### 2000s
*The War on Terrorism*

The Christian fundamentalists the OE originally backed to fight the Soviets begin attacking OE embassies in Alaska. The OE responds by pounding rural Alaska with cruise missiles. The Leader of the Christian fundamentalists orchestrates a massive retaliation on Istanbul, the largest city in the OE, causing 3,000 civilian deaths.

The OE reacts by occupying California, resulting in 100,000 civilian deaths, then invading Alaska, resulting in 6,000 civilian deaths, and launching hundreds of Predator drone strikes all over the

American states, killing thousands of innocent Americans.

Ottoman citizens were then utterly perplexed why Americans hated them.

# Defining Terrorism

Words have definitions, and that's kind of important to clear thinking. When words become divorced from their definitions. they become confusing, even dangerous, because they can then be used entirely for their emotional impact, which allows them to manipulate people. *Terrorism* is one of those words that is historically difficult to define.

Actually defining *terrorism* has been the great bugbear of the War on Terror. For years the UN has repeatedly failed to arrive at an internationally agreed-upon definition. Why? Because it is virtually impossible to find any definition of *terrorism* that does not exactly describe the actions of governments.

The United States Code resolves this little conundrum. The full definition in the US Code reads:

> terrorism, -n. (politically motivated violence perpetrated against noncombatant targets by subnational groups or clandestine agents, usually intended to influence an audience.)
> —US Code Title 22, Ch.38, Para.2656f(d)

By tacking three little words—"by subnational groups"—to their definition, suddenly it's not "terrorism" when the State does it... only when it's done by non-State agents.

So, Al Qaida is a terrorist organization without question. It's obvious. But by this definition, the Taliban were not a terrorist organization between 1996 and 2001 when they ruled the Islamic Emirate of Afghanistan. They only became one after Operation Enduring Freedom, when they were demoted to a "subnational group." On the other hand, by this definition, Irgun was a terrorist organization until the establishment of Israel in 1948 when they were absorbed into the Israeli Defense Forces.

You can see why finding a consistent definition is problematic—but there's another method by which an analyst can derive the meaning of a term. We can observe and examine the common usage. Let's take a look.

The Liberty Dollar we discussed in the previous chapter was dubbed *terrorism* by US Attorney Anne Tompkins, who stated, "Attempts to undermine the legitimate currency of this country are simply a unique form of domestic terrorism." The quote was repeated in the press release of the FBI's Charlotte, North Carolina, office. Recall that Tompkins affirmed that NotHaus's activities, "do not involve violence," but that they "represent a clear and present danger to the economic stability of this country."

In 2010 WikiLeaks achieved international attention with its release of thousands of classified diplomatic cables allegedly leaked by Bradley Manning. Among other crimes, WikiLeaks revealed that a Texas contractor was pimping little boys to Afghan cops. Many on the left and right, even in the State Department, were clamoring to have WikiLeaks declared a terrorist organization. Representative Peter King, the chairman of the House Committee on Homeland Security, argued that WikiLeaks should be classified as a terrorist organization because, "by doing that, we will be able to seize their funds and go after anyone who provides them help or contributions," even though WikiLeaks has never engaged in violence. They have only done digitally what any mainstream media outlet would do with documents leaked by whistleblowers. Incidentally, King was once an enthusiastic supporter of the Irish Republican Army, considered one of the world's most dangerous terrorist organizations at the time.

In 2011, Orlando, Florida, activists from the international grassroots group Food Not Bombs were dubbed dangerous "food terrorists" by the city's mayor, Buddy Dyer. You might think, with a label like that, that they were serving up anthrax or yellowcake, but no—they were just dishing out some good homemade vegetarian chili. The city of Orlando banned "group feedings" because the presence of homeless people was "detrimental to the aesthetic atmosphere of parks." In defiance of this ordinance, Food Not Bombs continued to hand out free food at Lake Eola Park week after week, resulting in the arrest of at least twenty-two civilly disobedient activists, including the group's co-founder Keith McHenry. A volunteer from Food Not Bombs responded: "We think that it's terrorism to arrest people for trying to share food with poor and hungry people." Silly activist... it's not "terrorism" when the *State* does it.

So, we've got economic terrorism, information terrorism, and food terrorism. What's the common thread? We certainly can't call these things violence, and other than serving them free food, they aren't targeting noncombatants. That leaves "politically motivated." The definition of *terrorism*, based on its observed usage, is just "premeditated political motivation by subnational groups or clandestine agents." In other words, "dissent," whether by competing with State services, exposing State malfeasance, or simply disobeying the State. If you try to take any politically motivated action, perhaps even attending a protest, and the State doesn't like it, you might be a terrorist.

# Fort Hood:

# Remember, Remember the 5<sup>th</sup> of November

On Thursday, November 5th, 2010, I was driving home when I heard over the radio the last line of a public statement from Barack Obama: "It's difficult enough when we lose these brave Americans in battles overseas. It is horrifying that they should come under fire at an Army base on American soil."

My heart sank, and suddenly it was 2001, on the 11th of September. Without any details, my mind produced the worst case scenario: gunfire and smoke... explosions and blood. And as I imagined the consequences of another terrorist attack, all I could think about was internment camps.

By the time I got the story, most of the facts of the shooting were known. Major Nidal Malik Hasan, an Army psychiatrist scheduled for deployment to Afghanistan, had opened fire on a Texas military base, screaming "Allahu Akbar" as he fired two handguns at fellow soldiers. He killed thirteen and injured thirty before he was taken down by a civilian officer. He is now alive, in critical condition. The greatest tragedy of the day was the loss of an unborn child inside the womb of a female officer.

> "We can only prevent the occurrence of evil if we are honest about its cause."
> —Stefan Molyneux

As details began coming to light, we started to see the character of a very conflicted man. His family reports that he'd joined the military believing he had a duty to serve his country. Yet he was outspoken about his opposition to the current conflict in Iraq and Afghanistan. He served for six years as an army psychiatrist at Walter Reed Army Medical Center. Yet he was frequently bullied, and his property was vandalized by other personnel because he was Muslim. He sought a discharge for several years, offered to repay the cost of his medical training, and hired a lawyer to help him find a way out, but with no success. Yet he gave presentations where he made statements radically outside the mainstream views of Muslims. Examining the trajectory of Major Hasan, we see a man on a downward spiral into violent extremism, and yet he gave his superior officers every possible indication that he was unstable. When the orders came for his deployment, and that internal contradiction was no longer reconcilable, he lashed out.

"The beginning of wisdom is to call things by their true name."
—Chinese Proverb

In the last article, I provided one definition of "terrorism" from the US Code that amounted to little more than State propaganda. Here's a better one:

terrorism, -n. (the calculated use of violence, or the threat of violence, against civilians in order to attain goals that are political or religious or ideological in nature; this is done through intimidation or coercion or instilling fear)
— Princeton WordNet

Most State definitions insert the word "unlawful" before "violence" to exclude their own acts of violence against civilians. They believe that costumes, flags, and badges change moral rules and somehow make violence virtuous. But a consistent attribute of all the definitions I found is that terrorism targets civilians, which is so clearly forbidden in Islam as to be beyond debate.

By any definition the attack on Fort Hood was not an act of terrorism. I am not defending Nidal Hasan's actions. I am merely calling them by their true name. Calling this *terrorism* waters down the true moral horror of willfully targeting civilians. This attack was an act of treason, which is already a capital crime. It should be investigated, tried, and punished as treason. Based on his own statements, Nidal Hasan should never have been permitted to serve in the military, which was his wish as well, but calling this *terrorism* is Orwellian newspeak where the emotional content of a word is more important than its definition. It is a kind of thought control. It changes the very definition to something more like "any subversive act by any Muslim for any reason."

Muslims are falling in lockstep into a reactionary campaign of condemnation. "We condemn terrorism!" "We condemn terrorism!" "We condemn terrorism!" This is not participation in a national discussion, but an act of self-defense.

"Freedom is the right to tell people what they do not want to hear."
—George Orwell

There is an environment of fear being achieved here. I am afraid to say what I am saying right now... and if you are Muslim, you are probably afraid to read it. We scramble to distance ourselves from any subversive act by any Muslim for any reason. This is motivated by fear, because we understand that we are civilians living under the subtle threat of tremendous violence. We understand, consciously or not, that speaking openly about evil is "thoughtcrime." We understand that our own government has declared war on an idea it has not clearly defined. And we wait for them to tell us what is permissible to say, what is permissible to think and what is permissible to believe, lest they declare war on us.

# Nidal Hasan: Terrorist or Hero?

Reports litter the Internet connecting Nidal Hasan with Imam Anwar al-Awlaki, an American Islamic scholar in Yemen who praised Hasan as a hero on a recent blog post. Emails intercepted by US intelligence confirm their contact, and the media is portraying him as the new Osama bin Laden. He wrote:

> Nidal Hassan is a hero. He is a man of conscience who could not bear living the contradiction of being a Muslim and serving in an army that is fighting against his own people... The heroic act of brother Nidal also shows the dilemma of the Muslim American community. Increasingly they are being cornered into taking stances that would either make them betray Islam or betray their nation... It is becoming more and more difficult to hold on to Islam in an environment that is becoming more hostile towards Muslims.

I'm not about to take that position, but I can understand the logic of both sides. The standard reasoning goes, if you are in favor of the war you must necessarily believe that the actions of the military are just. If the actions of the military are just, then they have the right to initiate violence on the opposition. If they have the right to initiate violence, then the defense of the opposition is illegitimate. If the defense of the opposition is illegitimate, then one who strikes against the military is a terrorist. To understand Imam Anwar's reasoning, all you have to do is reverse the first premise. If you are against the war, you must necessarily believe that the actions of the military are unjust. If the actions of the military are unjust, then the opposition has a right to defend themselves. If they have a right to defend themselves, then the military is a legitimate target. If the military is a legitimate target, then one who strikes against the military is a hero. That's the unfortunate dichotomy created by the initiation of violence. I'm not ready to call Nidal Hasan a terrorist *or* a hero, but I'd like to discuss two examples from recent news that describe what I think Major Hasan could have done that I would have condemned as terrorism, and would have praised as heroism.

Consider the story of the Eagle Bar published in the Huffington Post in September 2009. Patrons were sitting at the bar watching football when suddenly they heard a voice shout, "*Hit the ground!*" The lights switched on and in rushed roughly thirty cops barking orders with guns drawn. One of the bar patrons asked "Why?" and received the answer "Shut the fuck up!" The elderly man was targeted and forced face-down on the filthy floors. "No questions! Do what you're told or we'll arrest you!" The search and seizures began. Everything in everyone's pockets was taken. Drivers' licenses were put through a laptop screening. Du-wan Ray, the bar's manager, was handcuffed and overheard one officer say to another, "This is a lot more fun than raiding niggers with crack!" The officers high-fived each other. For almost two hours, sixty-two men were forced to lie face-down on the ground while the cops searched. The police didn't find one suspended license, one criminal prior—no drugs, no weapons, nothing. Not even a parking ticket. In the end, the men were ordered to leave the bar without their cell phones, wallets, and personal belongings. Not one arrest. Not one apology. When bar patrons asked why this had happened, one cop said, "I hate queers!" The Eagle was a gay bar.

Remember our definition of terrorism:

> terrorism, -n. (the calculated use of violence, or the threat of violence, against civilians in order to attain goals that are political or religious or ideological in nature; this is done through intimidation or coercion or instilling fear)
> — Princeton WordNet

What these men did was absolutely terrorism. Maybe they didn't blow themselves up in a café. Maybe they didn't fly planes into buildings. But they absolutely used calculated force, and the threat of force, against civilians through intimidation and instilling fear. These men should lose their badges, and they should serve time in prison. But this kind of tyranny is becoming all too common as soldiers home from war are ushered directly into the civilian police force, and police departments adopt military "crowd control" techniques. These thugs are drunk on power.

Imagine if, when entering a new Afghani village, an army unit forced all the men's faces in the dirt at gunpoint, robbed them, and, when no ties to any terrorist network could be confirmed and the civilian population was asking why this had happened, a solider replied, "I hate sand niggers." I have no doubt that, as a military psychiatrist, Nidal Hasan heard endless accounts like this from soldiers returning from war in need of his professional help. I'm sure he listened to these stories and in his heart of hearts he thought, "Those were my people." But imagine if Nidal Hasan himself had gone to Afghanistan and taken part in such a raid where violence and intimidation were used against innocent civilians without just cause. If he had done that, I would condemn him as a terrorist.

Now, consider the story of former Austin Police Department

rookie officer Ramon Perez, from *The Austin Chronicle:* He filed a civil lawsuit against the department, his former supervisors, and an APD psychologist, because he had been forced to resign based on his religious beliefs after he refused to use excessive force against a suspect. Perez disobeyed an order from senior police officer Robert Paranich to use his Taser on an elderly man because the man was not resisting arrest and could easily be subdued with lesser force. Perez said the man appeared to be in questionable health and a likely candidate for a heart attack. In such circumstances the Taser can be lethal. Perez successfully placed the man under arrest with no more force than soft-hand control, which proves the Taser would have been excessive. After the incident Sergeant Jesse Brown ordered him to report to APD psychologist Carol Logan for a "fit-for-duty review," which was used to justify his termination. Logan's 4-page report focused entirely on Perez's religious beliefs. She wrote: "Perez has a well-developed set of personal beliefs. These seem to be based primarily on his religious beliefs and it is obvious that he has spent a lot of time reflecting upon and developing these views." The report concludes that Perez, a nondenominational fundamentalist Christian, was so impaired by his moral convictions as to be unfit for duty. Perez was given a choice to resign or be fired, and chose to resign. Perez refused to comply with an unlawful order, and he argues that he was forced to resign, in violation of the First Amendment, after refusing to violate the rights of another.

Ramon Perez is a man whose moral convictions transcend the authority of the State. A man whose ultimate concern was his accountability to God. A Christian first and a police officer second. Ramon Perez is worthy of praise as a hero. I've heard from many well-intentioned police officers that corruption rises through the ranks in these departments, and men of true valor, such as Perez, are eclipsed by trigger-happy sadists eager to aim their new toys at you and me.

What if Nidal Hasan had followed in the footsteps of Ramon Perez, as all men of conscience should, and simply disobeyed? Just imagine if, when confronted with the contradiction between his moral convictions and his orders, he'd simply refused to comply. Maybe he would have been discharged after a psychological evaluation like Perez, or maybe he would have gone to prison for insubordination. Either way he would have retained his moral credibility. Imagine the impact if Nidal Hasan had instead written a book about his experience as a military psychiatrist, about his own internal struggle, and the moral conflict inside every soldier of conscience. The impact of such a book would have accomplished far more for the peace effort than the death of thirteen soldiers. If Nidal Hasan had done that, I would praise him as a hero.

# The Wrigleyville Bomb Plot Was
# FBI-Orchestrated, Not Jihad

There's an old saying amongst political activists: If you want to know who the undercover agent is, it's the guy advocating violence.

A 22-year-old Lebanese man was arrested by the FBI for attempting to detonate an improvised explosive device left in a trash can near Chicago's Wrigley Field during a Dave Matthews Band concert. Some have dubbed the attack a "jihadist plot" and an act of a "lone wolf terrorist." But Sami Samir Hassoun did not act alone. His terror cell consisted of two undercover FBI agents posing as financiers, and a longtime friend who turned out to be an FBI informant. In fact, the FBI were the ones who gave him the bomb, and paid him to deliver it, which raises the question, how much of the plot was their idea?

Special Agent in Charge Robert Grant assured the Chicago public after the arrest that they were never in any danger during the investigation, and the bomb was a dud the whole time. Although Grant declined to offer any specific details about Hassoun's motivations when interviewed by the Associated Press, clues appear in the 26-page criminal complaint filed against him. According to the complaint, Hassoun was carrying out a personal vendetta against Mayor Richard Daley, and far from being motivated by religion, he was seeking personal monetary and political gain.

Hassoun's friends describe him as not particularly religious, and he was very explicit with his FBI accomplices that his motivation was "not inspired by any religious ideology." One of the undercover agents told Hassoun that his motivation was "to change how our country [the United States] treats our people [the Arabs] back home," to which Hassoun responded, "Mine is a kind of different concept than this." Hassoun explained that his intention in attacking Chicago was to somehow gain political control of the city and its sources of revenue. In fact, Hassoun suggested that they release a fake attribution video to the media blaming a fictional jihadist organization as a scapegoat. He said, "Call it, 'the jihad in US.' Just make something up. You know? Just make it up, like, when you put it, all the heat is transferred to them."

Far from being concerned for the welfare of his fellow Arabs, one of his first ideas for a target was the Chicago Arabesque Festival, an event designed to celebrate the cultural heritage of the Arab world. He also realized that people would naturally suspect Islamic extremists if they chose a target that served alcohol, such as Sluggers World Class

Sports Bar, where the bomb was dropped, and suggested that they could bribe certain media personnel to blame the attack on Muslims. It may be worth pointing out that Hassoun's religion is never identified in the affidavit, and Lebanon is only half Muslim.

According to the complaint Hassoun's primary goal was to "foster a revolution in Chicago" specifically to unseat Mayor Daley, or force his resignation. His main grievance was apparently the mayor's weak security policies. He planned to foment fear in order to undermine the mayor's political support and paralyze commerce, presumably to coerce the city into increasing security. He told the undercover agents that his plan was to "take that Daley out and put some of our guys in." He floated the idea of cultivating a replacement candidate. It's not specified in the complaint who he's talking about, but this sounds more like the plan of a radical right-winger than an Islamic extremist.

Interestingly, Hassoun's initial plans were non-lethal, but designed to only incite fear. He suggested deploying multiple car bombs in different locations that would ignite and not explode. He conceived of a device that would appear like a toy, but when detonated, would expel informative pamphlets rather than causing injuries. In fact, while planning with the informant before the involvement of the undercover agents, Hassoun was very clear that whatever they chose to do, he didn't want to actually kill anyone. He told the informant, "No killing. There is no killing," according to the complaint.

It is unclear how much of the final plan was Hassoun's own and how much was instigated by the agents. Hassoun's attorney, Myron Auerbach, said he may claim entrapment: "My client didn't bring anything of his own making to the incident. Things were given to him." What is clear is that the agents promised him substantial monetary gain if he did carry out the attack. Starting in July the agents were paying Hassoun a monthly salary so that he could devote his full attention to the operation. They offered to provide him with a house and a nice car if he followed their instructions. And they discussed selling information about the bombing to the media. They provided him with equipment to run reconnaissance on the proposed target, transportation to and from the scene, and the bomb itself.

# Counter-Terrorism:
# How America Is Destroying Itself

At a Christmas tree-lighting ceremony in Portland, Oregon, another FBI–co-produced terror plot landed a young Muslim in custody, charged with "attempted use of a weapon of mass destruction." According to an affidavit detailing the sting operation, the bomb the FBI provided never contained any explosives, and they claim the public was never in any real danger.

Nineteen-year-old Mohamed Osman Mohamud allegedly made contact with an "unindicted associate" in northwest Pakistan known as "Abu Abdallah." Together they discussed Mohamed traveling overseas to engage in "violent jihad." Abu allegedly referred Mohamed to a second "unindicted associate" who went by "Abdul Hadi" to make travel arrangements, but this second contact was never made. Instead Mohamed was emailed by an undercover FBI agent impersonating an associate of Abdul Hadi. Together, Mohamed and two undercover agents posing as financiers spent months planning the attack.

Judging by the content of the FBI affidavit, Mohamed is not a sympathetic character. He had allegedly been committed to violence since the age of 15, and he apparently expressed glee at the notion of killing innocent civilians. In a video he prepared to explain his reasons for the attack, Mohamed said, "For as long as you threaten our security, your people will not remain safe. As your soldiers target our civilians, we will not help to do so. Do you think that you could invade a Muslim land, and we would not invade you?"

Mohamed's defense attorneys issued a public statement saying, "The information released by the government raises serious concerns about the government manufacturing a crime." They have asserted that he couldn't have accomplished the attack without their encouragement and financing. To avoid entrapment as a defense, the FBI must be able to show that Mohamed acted of his own volition and not at their instruction. Although the FBI recorded all their conversations on multiple recording devices during their investigation, the critical conversation where Mohamed allegedly asked to become "operational" was not recorded due to "technical problems."

FBI stings of this kind are becoming routine. An undercover agent posing as a financier approaches a potential patsy and provides him with equipment and money to fulfill his violent ambition. Once he takes the bait, the agent provides him with a fake bomb, and when he attempts to detonate the dud, he is arrested as a terrorist.

Waiting for the suspect to attempt to detonate a fake bomb, rather than busting him earlier in the operation leaves the prosecution wide open to an entrapment defense, and the news coverage severely compromises access to a fair trial. Members of the Portland Muslim community have argued that Mohamed was young enough that some kind of community intervention could have saved him from the extremist message he found on the Internet. In fact, after hitting a dead end with his contact in Pakistan, there's no guarantee Mohamed ever would have acted on his violent ambitions without help. But law enforcement has a perverse incentive to try to bust big cases instead of preventing them, because they make headlines, get promotions, and grow budgets. Ironically, headlines, promotions, and budgets are the primary problem with this strategy.

What's not commonly understood is that Al Qaida's primary goal is not mass murder, but economic damage. Mohamed alluded to this fact in his video when he said, "To those doubting the victory of Allah, then we say there's a lesson in the USSR for you." This rather obscure reference would be lost on most observers, but stands out like a lighthouse when one considers that Al Qaida's strategy against the US is identical to the Mujaheddin's strategy against the USSR in the 1980s.

Al Qaida cannot win militarily, just as the Mujaheddin could not hope to defeat the Soviet Union by battlefield victories alone. Instead, their strategy is to provoke the US into spending itself into insolvency. Using relatively inexpensive means, they can force the US to spend unsustainable amounts of money on counter-terrorism measures until the economic reality forces them to withdraw, or worse, collapse.

By the best estimates Al Qaida spent $500,000 on the September 11th attack, which cost the US more than $500 billion. The price tag on the 2009 underwear bomb was in the thousands, but in response, the US has spent over $300 billion on their new naked body scanners. This level of spending is unsustainable, as it was in the USSR. Even when an attack fails to do any actual damage, Al Qaida still succeeds in their economic goals.

The FBI's counter-terrorism strategy complements perfectly Al Qaida's economic strategy. After the FBI thwarted their own terror plot in Washington DC, the Metro Police announced new more expensive security procedures. After the FBI busted this recent plot, the Portland City Council is considering joining the FBI's Joint Terrorism Task Force. Now, thanks to the FBI, Al Qaida doesn't have to spend one thin dime tricking America into destroying itself with headlines, promotions, and budget increases.

# Condemning Terrorism

As a Muslim in America, I am constantly being asked to condemn terrorism. The implication being that if I don't condemn terrorism, or more accurately specific terrorists, I'm a bad American. So, everyone put down the flags and the history books for a second, because I think this deserves some deeper contemplation.

Remember our definition of terrorism:

> terrorism, -n. (the calculated use of violence, or the threat of violence, against civilians in order to attain goals that are political or religious or ideological in nature; this is done through intimidation or coercion or instilling fear)
> — Princeton WordNet

Now compare that with our definition of government:

> government, -n. (that entity which claims a monopoly on the legitimate use of violence in a given area)
> —Max Weber, *Politics as a Vocation*

By these definitions a government is a terrorist organization. An entity which claims a monopoly on the calculated use of violence, or the threat of violence, against civilians in a given area in order to attain goals that are political or religious or ideological in nature.

Viewed this way, a government is essentially just a terrorist organization that achieves a monopoly, and subjugates its people so successfully that overt violence is masked behind a successful public relations campaign.

This pushes me into an uncomfortable corner. If I consistently condemn terrorism, I must condemn the very concept of government, or at least this concept of government. That puts me in a radical political fringe, not only among Americans, but among Muslims—yet by any rational criterion I can use to determine who deserves my condemnation, this is true. I'll go where the evidence leads.

I condemn, in the most serious of terms, any and all initiation of violence, or threat of violence, against civilians to achieve political, religious, or ideological goals. What kind of sense would it make to say that I don't condemn it when it's perpetrated by those dressed in the right costume, wearing the right badge, or waving the right flag?

# Chapter Four: Authoritarian Sociopathy

## Power and Obedience

For those interested in the science behind authoritarian sociopathy no studies are more poignant, or more chilling in their ramification than the Milgram Experiment and the Stanford Prison Experiment. But their sentiment was perhaps best expressed by Thomas Jefferson in an often-overlooked passage of the Declaration of Independence:

> all experience hath shewn, that mankind are more disposed to suffer, while evils are sufferable, than to right themselves by abolishing the forms to which they are accustomed.

After World War II the world stood in shock and horror as the details of the Holocaust came to light. Jews, Gypsies, homosexuals, and virtually anyone deemed an enemy of the state were put to death by the Nazis. The constant, even robotic refrain from these soldiers during the Nuremberg Trials was "I was just following orders." As the world cried, "Never again!" Stanley Milgram, a Yale University psychologist asked, "How did this happen in the first place?" The Milgram Experiment was designed to measure the willingness of otherwise psychologically healthy people to obey the unethical orders of an authority figure. His shocking results were published in the 1974 book *Obedience to Authority: An Experimental View.*

In the Milgram Experiment, participants were divided into "teachers" and "learners," and placed in separate rooms. They could communicate, but could not see each other. The experimenter instructed the "teachers" to read questions to the "learners" and, if they answered incorrectly, to administer an electro-shock of ever-increasing voltage. The "teachers" were unaware that the "learners" were actually plants and the electro-shocks were fake. The "teachers" were the actual subjects in the experiment. After a few volt increases the "learner" began to object, to bang on the walls and complain about a heart condition. After some time, the "learner" would go silent. If the subject asked to stop the experiment for any reason, he was given a succession of verbal prods by the experimenter: "Please continue," "The experiment requires that you continue," "You must continue," etc.

Most went right on pushing the buttons after being told that they would not be held responsible.

Psychologists predicted that only 1% of subjects would administer a lethal shock, but were utterly astonished when 65% administered the experiment's massive maximum 450 volts, even though every subject expressed some level of objection in doing so. Some began to laugh nervously. Others offered to refund the money they had been paid for participating in the experiment. Some exhibited signs of extreme stress once they heard the screams of pain coming from the learner. But the vast majority were willing to administer a lethal jolt of electricity to a complete stranger based upon nothing but the verbal prodding of a scientist in a lab coat. None of those who refused to administer the deadly shock insisted that the experiment itself be terminated.

The Stanford Prison Experiment was a study conducted by Stanford University psychology professor Philip Zimbardo to determine the psychological effects of prison life. Participants were screened to be otherwise stable and psychologically healthy, and assigned randomly as either "prisoner" or "guard" to live in a two-week-long prison simulation in the basement of the Stanford psychology building. Guards were given uniforms, mirrored glasses to prevent eye contact, and wooden batons meant only to establish status. Prisoners were dressed in smocks and addressed only by the numbers they were issued. Guards were instructed to keep a fixed schedule, and to try to make the prisoners feel powerless, but not to physically harm them.

The experiment was halted after only six days.

After a prisoner revolt on the second day, guards began to display cruel, even sadistic behavior. A system of punishment soon followed that included spraying disobedient prisoners with fire extinguishers, depriving them of bedding or restroom privileges, forcing them to go nude, and locking them in "solitary confinement" in a dark closet. On the other hand, after the initial revolt, and a brief hunger strike, prisoners developed submissive attitudes, accepting physical abuse and readily following orders from the guards to inflict punishments on each other. They even engaged in horizontal discipline to keep each other in line. One prisoner began showing signs of mental breakdown after only 36 hours. Yet everyone one of them stayed, even though they were all made aware that they could stop the experiment at any time. As Zimbardo explained, both prisoners and guards had fully internalized their new identities.

Zimbardo ultimately halted the experiment when he realized that his judgment had been compromised by being sucked into his role as "Prison Superintendent," and he'd allowed abuse to continue that could be considered torture. His recent book, *The Lucifer Effect:*

*Understanding How Good People Turn Evil*, details his findings and how they relate to the torture and prisoner abuse at Abu Ghraib.

Ethical concerns raised by these results have made it illegal to repeat these experiments. In fact, under current ethical guidelines, the State makes it very difficult to study the psychology of power and authority at all. Still, there have been some more recent studies that flesh out the findings of these classic experiments. In this chapter we will be discussing the effect of power on honesty, compassion, and integrity.

What is clear to me from these experiments is that human nature is neither good nor evil, but essentially adaptive. If you take an otherwise good person and invent for them a role that incentivizes evil, they will adjust to their new circumstances. And a person who internalizes "obedience to authority" as a core personality trait will become capable of the worst forms of murder, and tolerant of the worst forms of abuse.

# Power and Deception

Because of the new legal limitations, more recent experiments on authority are not as dramatic as previous ones, but the implications of their results are no less startling.

Dana Carney is a professor at Columbia University. She conducted an experiment intended to discover whether "leaders" and "subordinates" experience the same physiological response to lying. She found that power not only makes lying easier, but pleasurable.

Participants from diverse backgrounds were subjected to personality tests that identified them as "leaders" or "subordinates." In reality the selection was random, but the fake test allowed them to believe their assignment was somehow deserved. Those randomly designated as "leaders" were each placed in a large office with an executive desk, while others randomly designated as "subordinates" were placed in small windowless cubicles. Both groups were given an hour of busy-work. After this, they engaged in a 10-minute mock negotiation over compensation.

After the mock negotiation, half the "leaders" and half the "subordinates" were given a hundred-dollar bill by an experimenter. They were told that they could keep the money if they convinced a second experimenter that they were one of the subjects from the half of the group who hadn't been given any money during the closing interview. The second experimenter did not know which subjects had the money and which didn't.

For most people, lying elicits negative emotions, cognitive impairment, physiological stress, and nonverbal behavioral cues, all of which can be measured. Video of the interviews was reviewed to identify behavioral cues, such as fidgeting or increasing rate of speech. Saliva samples were tested for increases in the stress hormone cortisol. Tests of reaction time were conducted on the computer to demonstrate cognitive impairment. A mood survey assessed participants' emotional states during the experiment.

By every measure, liars from the "subordinate" class exhibited all the indicators of deception. They reported negative emotions, demonstrated cognitive impairment and increased stress levels, and exhibited behavioral cues associated with lying. Liars from the "leader" class exhibited the exact opposite: by every measure, they were indistinguishable from truth-tellers. In fact, it was discovered that they enjoyed reduced levels of stress and increased cognitive function, and reported positive emotions. Only "subordinates" reported feeling bad about lying.

Professor Carney speculates that authority could have a similar impact on other unethical behavior, with similar physiological responses, such as cheating, stealing, exploitation, reckless behavior, and even political corruption. She concludes, "Power will lead to increases in intensity and frequency of lying."

In other words, lying comes easier, and may be inherently more pleasurable, to those in a position of authority, even fake authority. Also, positions of authority not only attract dishonest people, but actually incentivize dishonesty.

So, going back to the Stanford Prison Experiment, being a prison guard not only induces cruel and sadistic behavior, but also makes it easier to lie to cover it up. Returning to the Milgram Experiment, being in a position of subordination induces a willingness to follow unethical orders. And the Columbia University Experiment shows that being in a position of authority may make it easier, even pleasurable, to give unethical orders in the first place.

# Power and Compassion

Psychologist Gerben A. van Kleef from the University of Amsterdam collaborated with colleagues from UC Berkeley to conduct an experiment designed to identify how power influences someone's emotional reactions to the suffering of others.

Unlike the previous experiments we've discussed, where participants were randomly selected for "high-power" and "low-power" roles, in this experiment, participants from diverse backgrounds filled out a questionnaire about their own sense of power in their actual lives. Subjects were randomly paired off to take turns sharing stories in which they experienced great pain, or emotional suffering.

During the exchange both participants were hooked up to electrocardiogram (ECG) machines that measured stress levels, and after the exchange they all filled out a second questionnaire describing their own emotional experience, and what they perceived of their partner's emotional experience.

The results were unmistakable.

For starters, increased stress readings in the storyteller correlated with increased stress readings in low-power listeners, but not in high-power listeners. In other words, low-power individuals respond to the suffering of others with emotional reciprocity, but high-power individuals experience greater emotional regulation, or detachment.

According to self-reporting after the experiment, high-power individuals feel less compassion than do low-power individuals, as might be expected. But there were other interesting results in the post-analysis. High-power listeners were unmotivated to empathize with their partner. In other words, they saw the emotions of others, but just didn't care. This could explain why high-power listeners don't experience emotional reciprocity: They are simply indifferent to other people's suffering.

Also, storytellers with high-power listeners reported higher distress than storytellers with low-power listeners. This could indicate that high-power individuals suffer in their interpersonal relationships because their lack of compassion actually exacerbates the suffering of those around them.

After the experiment, researchers inquired about whether participants would like to stay in touch with their partners. As you might expect, the low-power subjects liked the idea, but the high-power subjects didn't.

Now... let's speculate.

In the Stanford Prison Experiment we saw subjects randomly

appointed as "high-power" individuals torture subjects randomly appointed as "low-power" individuals. Van Kleef's research may explain why: Once the subjects of the study were given a taste of power, they simply no longer experienced reciprocal emotions with those who were powerless. And worse, the lack of compassion of the "guards" would have exacerbated the suffering experienced by the "prisoners."

How can we apply these findings to the Milgram Experiment scenario, where an authority orders a subordinate to murder a stranger? We already know that 65% of subordinates in that experiment obeyed orders that they viewed as unethical. In this case the authority is the "high-power" individual, the subordinate is the "low-power" individual, and the stranger is the one who suffers. So, we can speculate that the authority will feel less compassion for the suffering of the victim, which would make giving the lethal order easier for him (maybe even pleasurable). But we can also reason that the authority is less likely to feel compassion for the emotional distress of the subordinate. That means that the person making the life-or-death decision is the one most cut off from its consequences.

But here's where it gets sick: The subordinate, a "low-power" individual, has no such emotional detachment. As we saw in the Milgram Experiment, some of the subordinates "exhibited signs of extreme stress." The subordinate is stuck in the impossible position of both being conditioned to obey the authority, and empathizing with the victim. Is it any wonder we see high instances of suicide and post-traumatic stress disorder among soldiers, but not among the ranking officers who give them their orders?

# Power and Hypocrisy

It has become almost a cliché that the most outspoken anti-gay politicians are in fact closet homosexuals themselves, and the champions of "traditional family values" are frequently engaged in extramarital affairs. Nothing is more common than the fiscal conservative who demands ridiculous luxuries at the taxpayers' expense, or the anti-war progressive who takes campaign donations from the military industrial complex. Well, now it seems there's some science behind the hypocrisy of those in power.

Joris Lammers, from Tilburg University, and Adam Galinsky of the Kellogg School of Management have conducted a battery of experiments designed to test how having a sense of power influenced a person's moral standards, specifically whether or not they were likely to behave immorally while espousing intolerance for the behavior of others. In each of five experiments, the method of inducing a powerful feeling and the method of determining these double standards was different, but in every one the results were the same. Powerful people judge others more harshly, but cheat more themselves. What's especially interesting is their last experiment, where distinguishing between legitimate power and illegitimate power garnered the opposite results.

The first experiment was designed to determine the discrepancy between the subjects' expressed standards and their actual behavior. As in previous experiments, subjects were randomly assigned to a high-power or low-power class. To induce these feelings "high-power" subjects were asked by experimenters to recall an experience where they'd felt a sense of power. Meanwhile, "low-power" subjects were asked by experimenters to recall an experience where they felt powerless. Each subject was asked to rate how egregious a moral infraction they considered cheating. Then they were given an opportunity to cheat at dice. They were promised some number of lottery tickets equal to the roll of two dice, and then allowed to self-report their roll. The high-power subjects reported that they considered cheating a higher moral infraction than low-power subjects, but were also more likely to cheat themselves.

In the second experiment, participants were made to conduct a mock-government. Half were randomly given high-power roles in which they gave orders, and half were randomly given low-power roles in which they took orders. Then each group was asked about their feelings regarding minor common traffic violations, such as speeding, or rolling through stop signs. As expected, high-power subjects were more likely to give themselves permission to bend the rules if they were running late for an important meeting, but less likely to afford other drivers the same leniency.

In the third experiment, participants were divided as in the first experiment, by either recalling a personal experience where they felt powerful or powerless. Then each group was asked to describe their feelings about minor common tax evasions, such as not declaring freelance income. As expected, high-power subjects were more likely to bend the rules for themselves, but less likely to concede similar exceptions to others.

In the fourth experiment the sense of power was manipulated in an unusual way. All participants were asked to fill out a series of word puzzles, half of which contained high-power words such as "authority," and half featuring low-power words such as "subjugation." Then all participants were asked about their feelings regarding keeping a stolen bike that had been found abandoned in the road. As in all experiments, even with such a minor insignificant power disparity, those in the high-power group were more likely to say they would keep the bike, but also that others had an obligation to seek out the rightful owner, or turn the bike over to the police.

The fifth and final experiment yielded, by far, the most interesting results, and it is my hope that this is the direction this type or research takes in the future. The feeling of power was induced as it was in the first and third experiments, where participants were asked to describe experiences of power in their own lives, with one important distinction: In this experiment, the "high-power" class was divided into two groups, one of which was asked to describe an event in which they felt their power was legitimate and deserved, and another asked to describe a situation in which power was illegitimate and undeserved.

The hypocrisy results found in the previous four experiments emerged only when high-power subjects viewed their power as legitimate. Those who viewed their power as illegitimate actually gave the opposite results, a sort of anti-hypocrisy, which researchers dubbed "hypercrisy." They were harsher about their own transgressions, and more lenient toward others'.

This discovery could be the silver bullet that society has been searching for to put down the werewolf of political corruption. The researchers speculate that the vicious cycle of power and hypocrisy could be broken by attacking the legitimacy of power, rather than the power itself. As Lammers and Galinsky write in their conclusion:

> A question that lies at the heart of the social sciences is how this status-quo [power inequality] is defended and how the powerless come to accept their disadvantaged position. The typical answer is that the state and its rules, regulations, and monopoly on violence coerce the powerless to do

so. But this cannot be the whole answer...

Our last experiment found that the spiral of inequality can be broken, if the illegitimacy of the power-distribution is revealed. One way to undermine the legitimacy of authority is open revolt, but a more subtle way in which the powerless might curb self enrichment by the powerful is by tainting their reputation, for example by gossiping. If the powerful sense that their unrestrained self enrichment leads to gossiping, derision, and the undermining of their reputation as conscientious leaders, then they may be inspired to bring their behavior back to their espoused standards. If they fail to do so, they may quickly lose their authority, reputation, and—eventually—their power.

In this chapter we have seen that those given power are more likely to lie, cheat, and steal with impunity while also being harsher in their judgments of others for doing the same things. We have seen that those given power feel less compassion for the suffering of others, and are even capable of the torture and murder of innocent people. What's perhaps most disturbing is that we have seen that these sociopathic tendencies have been fostered in otherwise psychologically healthy people. In other words, the problem is not that sociopaths are drawn to positions of authority, but that positions of authority draw out the sociopath in everyone. This final experiment offers some hope that authoritarian sociopathy can not only be stopped, but driven into reverse, not by violence or revolution, but simply by undermining the sense of legitimacy.

# Chapter Five: Voluntaryism

## Welcome to America: You've Been Lied To

On the website of the United States Citizenship and Immigration Service (USCIS) is a document titled "Learn About the United States: Quick Civics Lessons for the Naturalization Test." Native-born Americans undergo fourteen years of indoctrination, so in order to bring immigrants up to speed, the State subjects them to a simplified, highly propagandized version of American history. As a result, many immigrants enter American society with a false sense of utopianism, only to be disappointed by the rude awakening of actual life in America.

As a public service, here's a guide to the top ten misrepresentations that appear in the USCIS document:

**1) The United States has a long history of welcoming immigrants.**

Anti-immigrant sentiment goes all the way back in US history. Benjamin Franklin wrote that German immigrants were too stupid to learn English, and that their "swarthy complexion" would dilute "the pure white people" who settled colonial Pennsylvania. Anti-Catholic rhetoric also goes back to the colonial period, but it reached its peak in the 1840s when huge numbers of Irish immigrants were accused of greater loyalty to the Pope than to the US government, and of conspiratorial ambitions to spread medieval theocracy. Sound familiar? Chinese, Italian, and Polish immigration were all opposed by American labor unions, who feared losing jobs to the flood of unskilled workers willing to work for lower wages. In fact, the original intent of minimum wage laws was to exclude immigrants from the labor market. Every immigrant population that has come to America has been met with fear and hate.

**2) The United States signed treaties with American Indian tribes to move them to reservations.**

While technically true in some cases, this completely ignores a long and violent history of persecution and genocide against the Native Americans. Policies of "Indian Removal" began almost the moment colonists set foot in the New World, including mass hangings, intentional infection with smallpox, and the deliberate destruction of flora and fauna used by indigenous people for food. The systematic extermination of buffalo resulted in wide-scale starvation. The

Removal Act of 1830 forced the relocation of tens of thousands of Native Americans westward, often resulting in long death marches. Reservations were created by the Indian Appropriations Act of 1851. Tribes were scattered from their ancestral homes and concentrated into small parcels of land. Children were taken from their families, stripped of their way of life, and forced into manual labor. Clergy were stationed on reservations to teach Christianity. Even by conservative estimates, the Native American population has been reduced 95% from what it was prior to European contact.

### 3) The Constitution is the "supreme law of the land." Federal powers are restricted to those described in the Constitution.

Recently, when asked about the Constitutionality of Obama's healthcare bill, Democratic Congressman Jim Clyburn told Judge Andrew Napolitano, "Most of what we do in Washington is not authorized by the Constitution." A rare moment of honesty. The fact is, most of the laws on the books do not stand up to Constitutional rigor, and there is no golden age of Constitutionally limited government in our past. The federal government is, and always has been, exactly as large as it can get away with being. George Bush started a war without a formal declaration; Franklin D. Roosevelt authorized the Japanese internment camps; Woodrow Wilson established the Federal Reserve; Abraham Lincoln suspended habeas corpus; John Adams made it a crime to criticize government officials... As Lysander Spooner put it, the Constitution has either authorized tyranny, or has been powerless to prevent it.

### 4) The Civil War was fought to abolish slavery.

Most Northerners did not oppose slavery. In fact, Lincoln explicitly supported slavery in his first inaugural address. Many Southerners favored staying in the Union specifically because slavery was Constitutionally protected, while the volatility of a new Confederacy made it unclear whether slavery would continue in the South. Lincoln was a political novice whose campaign was bankrolled by Northern industrialists. They aimed to hike taxes on the South to subsidize industry in the North. Southern states felt bullied by the Northern majority and withdrew from the Union democratically. The war cry of the North was not "Free the slaves," but "Preserve the Union." The Emancipation Proclamation only freed the slaves in Confederate states, not in the North. Lincoln called it a "war measure," because it allowed free slaves to join the Union Army. Together with a draft—another form of involuntary servitude—this gave him the manpower to win the war. The 13th Amendment, which abolished chattel slavery, was supported by a majority of the Southern states. Every other country in the New World ended slavery without violence, with the exception of the Haitian Revolution, which was a slave revolt, not a civil war. The Civil War was essentially a very bloody tax revolt followed by a brilliant public relations campaign.

### 5) The federal government has the power to print money.

The US Treasury does not print money. In 1913 the monopoly privilege to print money was granted to the Federal Reserve, which was devised by a cartel of international bankers, not by Congress. The name itself is a fraud. The Federal Reserve is no more federal than Federal Express: It's a private cartel. Neither is it a reserve: There is no gold; there is no silver. They print a baseless paper note. Its only value is derived from legal tender laws that obligate its use. In reality a dollar is not a measure of value, but a measure of the National debt owed to the Federal Reserve. It is a central bank, which was bitterly opposed by the drafters of the Constitution. The founders recognized the importance of honest currency, which is why Article I, Section 10 reads, "No State shall... make any Thing but gold and silver Coin a Tender in Payment of Debts."

### 6) President Roosevelt's "New Deal" rescued America from the Great Depression.

The New Deal is cheered by policy-makers to this day, but economists now argue that it actually prolonged the Great Depression, and disproportionately hurt the poor. The upper class insiders actually profited immensely by loading up on debt during the boom of the 1920s, anticipating the crash, and then paying off their loans after inflation had devalued the currency. Meanwhile federal taxes tripled, primarily excise taxes levied on everyday things like chewing gum, soft drinks, phone service, and electricity. The financial burden of the New Deal programs fell disproportionately on the lower class that they purported to help. While a few jobs were created by direct spending, a greater number of jobs were destroyed by excessive taxing. Further, the majority of the spending did not go to the poorest of the poor, who were already overwhelmingly Democratic voters, but instead went to swing states, trying to buy political support for Roosevelt's reelection.

### 7) The "rule of law" means that our leaders must obey the law. No person is above the law.

When George Bush's daughter was charged with underage drinking, the comment from the White House was that they wanted to "keep it a family matter." Yet a less connected child would likely serve time in jail. The Obama administration is full of tax cheats. Dick Cheney shoots a hunting buddy in the face and nothing happens. Al Gore is accused of sexually assaulting a masseuse and nothing happens. Soldiers torture. Police speed and park illegally. Well-connected bankers rip off the taxpayer for billions. Justice is for sale. The "rule of law" is a nice idea for fairy tales, but in reality, laws are written by men, interpreted by men, implemented by men, and broken by men. There is no way to escape the rule of men... corrupt, flawed, power-hungry men.

### 8) The economic system of the United States is capitalism.

The economy may once have resembled capitalism somewhat, but it doesn't anymore. Capitalism is essentially a system of private property rights where goods are voluntarily exchanged in a free market. In the American system, licenses, permits, patents, and regulations are all coercive elements that hinder the free exchange of goods. Some call it a "mixed economy," meaning it contains elements of both a free market and a centrally planned economy. A more accurate term would be "corporatism." Big corporations cartelize to pool influence and collude with the government to monopolize industries and legislate competition out of the market. A corporation is a legal fiction—a file drawer someplace, regarded as a legal entity distinct from its members, who enjoy a special relationship with the State in which members have "limited liability," and are not fully accountable for the damages caused by their decisions. That is the very definition of *fascism*—the material success of capitalism colluding with the legal immunity of Statism.

### 9) The President commands the armed forces, but only Congress has the power to declare war.

Congress has not declared war since 1941 when America entered WWII. The Korean War, Vietnam, Desert Storm, the Iraq War, and now the ongoing War on Terror have all been undeclared unConstitutional wars. The framers of the Constitution denied the President the power to declare war to prevent the formation of a standing army, which they understood would be detrimental to American liberty. In fact, Article I, Section 8 limits war funding to no longer than two years.

Today we have exactly what the framers feared, and the military industrial complex that President Eisenhower warned us against. Basically it works like this: Huge corporations get lucrative government contracts to produce military equipment. If there is no war, there is no need for those contracts, so they have huge lobbying budgets to make sure we are in perpetual conflict. Congress is then put in the impossible position of "representing" people who are against the war, while taking huge sums of money from the corporations that depend on it. So they are more than happy to abdicate their responsibility to the President.

**10) The government works for the people. In the United States, the authority to govern comes from the consent of the people, who are the highest power.**

The Declaration of Independence states that "Governments are instituted among men, deriving their just powers from the consent of the governed." A recent Rasmussen poll of voters nationwide found that 61% said they don't believe the government has the necessary consent described in the Declaration of Independence; and 70% believed that government and corporations collude in ways that hurt the people. The power of the government doesn't come from the consent of the governed, it comes from the barrel of the gun. It comes from the militarization of police, and the largest military in human history. Think you're the highest power? Just try not paying your taxes.

# What's a Vote Worth?

It's that season again, when the tax cattle come out to elect their new masters, and stuff their suggestion box. I try to stay out of it, mainly because I just find the whole thing so humiliating, but also because so often when I do vote, I find myself being seduced into voting for things that, once implemented, I regret supporting.

People get really upset—red-in-the-face angry!—when I admit that I'm not that enthusiastic about voting. Especially since I spend so much time reading, writing, and demonstrating about political issues. Inevitably a cavalcade of thought-terminating clichés is trotted out whenever I try to explain myself. And I think that's pretty interesting. Whenever I see disproportionate anger in response to harmless action (or in this case, inaction), it suggests to me that we're not talking about the action itself—we're talking about a symbol, a sacred cow. We're talking about an intellectual idol, a fundamentally superstitious process of anxiety management that I am disrupting by not participating, and by raising the wrong questions.

So, I submit my humble attempt to explain why I'm not voting. Let's start with some numbers:

In the 2008 presidential race, the top three vote-getters were Barack Obama, John McCain, and Ralph Nader. Barack Obama's campaign spent $513,557,218 and received 69,498,215 votes (22% of the population). John McCain's campaign spent $346,666,422 and received 59,948,240 votes (19% of the population). Ralph Nader's campaign spent $4,187,628 and received 738,720 votes (less than 1% of the population). These numbers are from the Federal Election Commission.

What's immediately clear is that these elections do not represent the will of the majority, and the elected officials are not representative of the majority, because the majority doesn't vote. Currently it's not possible to determine to what degree this represents apathy or disapproval. Until "None of the Above" appears on the ballot, it's all nonsense. But here's what's interesting to me: Altogether, these campaigns spent a total of $864,411,268 and received 130,185,175 votes, for an average of $6.64 per ballot cast. Measured this way, I have already contributed more to political campaigns through monetary donations than every potential vote I could cast for the rest of my life. If you consider time value, I have probably accomplished more in the big picture by writing this article than I would by casting my vote. It's important to keep in mind that voting is not free. Nothing is free. There is an opportunity cost to everything. All the time you spend registering to vote, researching the propositions, debating with friends, looking up your polling location, and driving down to drop your suggestion in the box is time you didn't spend doing something more beneficial, and potentially something with greater impact on the political system.

In theory the purpose of voting is to express our will to government, and the purpose of government is to protect our civil liberties. Increasingly, especially for Muslims, voting is not merely an act of civic engagement, but an act of self-defense. See, there are actually two kinds of voting. The majority, whether they acknowledge it or not, vote in order to impose their will on others through the coercive force of the State, which is unconscionable. Still, some vote in order to prevent the will of others from being imposed upon them.

In the last decade we've seen control of the political apparatus swing completely from right to left, but still the same problems persist and expand. The people elected a Republican President who promised a humble foreign policy with no nation-building, and they received eight years of the complete opposite. Then they elected a Democrat President who promised to undo the worst of the damage, only to give us more of the same, and escalate the erosion of liberty.

We now have a government that arrests us without charges, imprisons us without trial, taps and tracks us without warrants, and, if we're really special, authorizes our assassination based on secret evidence without any judicial or congressional oversight. And all this only sets precedents for future administrations to push the line farther. I really don't think these are the people we should be looking toward to protect our civil liberties.

Instead, Americans should be looking to their own voluntary institutions. Those desiring government oversight would be better served donating $6.64 to CopBlock or Downsize DC than trying to cultivate a principled politician to vote for. Those desperate for an honest monetary policy would be better served investing in Shire Silver or the *Silver Circle* movie, than campaigning for anti-Fed bills. Those concerned about the erosion of liberty should be contributing to organizations that protect them, not begging the institution that destroys them.

If you truly care about the future of this society, it's time to allocate time and money to those organizations that are actually doing some good in this world. Because voting only gives us the illusion of taking action, while in reality accomplishing absolutely nothing.

# The Subject of Taxes

Tax season again. That magical time of year when, with fear in my heart, I mail my income extortion papers to the violent gang who steals my property under threat of violence. And now that it's all over, my mood has gone from fear to grief as I contemplate the uses these thugs will find for my "fair share." How much of my wealth will be used to pay the salaries of the bureaucrats who tap our phones? How much will be used to arm the boots who demand our papers, and invade our homes? How much will be used to terrorize quiet families and distant sands? How much blood is on my hands? If I were a braver man, I would refuse. But at least I am still free enough to expose the nature of the gang.

There is a wisdom in the subtle distinction between a "subject" and a "citizen." By the simplest legal definition, *subject* simply means "not exempt from tax," but politically, a subject is "a person who owes allegiance to a nation." A citizen is "a person who owes allegiance to a nation and is entitled to protection by and from the government." So, to be a citizen and not a subject, there must be a social contract where one exchanges allegiance for protection. To be clear, I don't believe any such contract exists. If it does, please tell me where I can read it. Nonetheless, the distinction rests upon whether or not we are entitled to protection by and from the government. Consider these:

June 27, 2005, in the case of *Castle Rock* v. *Gonzales*, the Supreme Court voted 7-to-2 that citizens did not have a Constitutional right to police protection.

February 22, 1989, in the case of *Deshaney* v. *Winnebago City Social Services*, the court ruled that there is "no duty on the State to provide members of the general public with adequate protective services."

December 21, 1981, in the case of *Warren* v. *District of Columbia*, the court ruled, "it is a fundamental principle of American law that a government and its agents are under no general duty to provide public services, such as police protection."

The list of cases goes all the way back to the 1800s. American courts have ruled over and over that government has no obligation to protect you or provide you with any services. Here's why: If the government had any legal obligation, it could be held liable when it failed. So instead, protection is regarded as a collective right, not an individual right. Can you imagine if I ran an insurance company this way? You pay me your insurance premium month after month and then when you file a claim, I respond, "Well, I don't actually have any obligation to cover your damages because this isn't 'individual' insurance, it's 'collective' insurance. The majority of our clients didn't have an accident." Bollocks! Imagine if you broke some arbitrary law and got hauled into court and you argued to the judge, "Well, I don't actually have any individual obligation to obey these laws. Americans 'collectively' obey the law." You'd be in a jail cell in about 30 seconds. But the government gets away with it because they have the monopoly on violence.

No liability, ergo no obligation. No obligation, ergo no valid contract. No valid social contract, ergo you are a subject, not a citizen. We are American subjects, not American citizens.

They even refer to us as subjects in their own documents. Here's Executive Order #6102, where President Roosevelt confiscated gold and silver that Americans owned right out of their safety deposit boxes:

> I, as President do declare that the national emergency still exists; that the continued private hoarding of gold and silver by subjects of the United States poses a grave threat to peace, equal justice, and well-being of the United States; and that appropriate measures must be taken immediately to protect the interest of our people. Therefore, pursuant to the above authority, I hereby proclaim that such gold and silver holdings are prohibited...

Roosevelt correctly refers to the legal residents of the United States as "subjects," not "citizens." Perhaps because he understands that in addition to not being entitled to protection by the government... we are not entitled to protection *from* the government.

# Black Market Secession

If any legacy is left of Abraham Lincoln's presidency, it's not the abolition of slavery, or the preservation of the Union. It is the solidification in the mind of everyone for generations that the Union was not a consensual association, and that leaving it carried violent consequences. Like a battered housewife afraid to divorce her brutal husband, whenever any whispering of secession sneaks into public conversation, someone inevitably says something like, "You can't do that—they'll just roll in tanks!" It's never a moral argument or a pragmatic argument; these are the exclusive property of the secessionists. Always, it is an argument from catastrophe. Every American understands on some level that the Union is held together by military aggression. The government doesn't care if you consent.

Since June 2008 the polling organization Rasmussen has conducted monthly national telephone surveys of likely voters that illustrate what I'm talking about:

In April 2009, only 11% of voters said they favored secession in their state, and only 22% said they even believed states had a right to secede from the Union. In June 2010, that went down to 10% in favor of secession and 18% who believed states had a right to secede.

In February 2010, just 21% of voters nationwide said they believed the government actually had the necessary consent of the governed described in the Declaration of Independence. In August 2011, only 17% of voters believed the federal government had the consent of the governed.

So, rounding the numbers, we see about 8 in 10 Americans are potential secessionists in the form of non-consent, but only about 1 in 10 would actually favor secession. In other words, about 7 in 10 Americans "are more disposed to suffer, while evils are sufferable," as the Declaration of Independence describes. That's a rough analysis, but it makes my point.

It's just a fact: When you prohibit a product or service for which there is a demand, it inevitably results in black market activity. So, what happens when independence is a crime? Only criminals will have independence. It is an inescapable law of nature; when force is overt, resistance is clandestine. If the American people are intimidated and afraid to publicly advocate secession, rising dissatisfaction with government will manifest in black market secession. In our analysis, 7 out of 10 Americans do not consent, and do not openly support secession. So, where's the black market? I think I found it.

The results of a Federal Deposit Insurance Corporation (FDIC) report were released that found—Brace yourself, because it is painfully obvious!: "When people believe the taxes they are required to pay are reasonable and the political leaders tend to spend their tax dollars wisely, tax compliance rises, and vice versa." I don't know about you, but I'm sure glad tax dollars were spent figuring that out. When dissatisfaction with government rises, and independence is not an option, the black market response is tax evasion, or economic secession.

The report found that 25.6% of US households were either "unbanked" or "underbanked"—whatever "underbanked" means. They also found that the paper currency in circulation, meaning not held in deposit anywhere, has risen 13.3% in two years, while the growth in electronic payment methods should result in a decrease in paper currency and increase in digital currency. These signal an increase in cash-only, untaxed, undeclared economic activity. The result being, according to the FDIC, that tax revenues at federal, state, and local levels are falling significantly faster than one would predict based on the economic conditions alone. Increases in taxes and onerous regulations only further erode public consent, galvanize public support for secession, and further enrich the black market.

People generally conceive of the black market as the underground sale of "illegal" products, like selling raw milk in Amish country. But increasingly it's not the product that the government objects to, it's the transaction itself. It's being called "the gray market." Not quite black because the products are generally legal to sell, buy, and consume, but not quite white, because the sale takes place in an untaxed, unregulated counter-economy.

It's called *agorism*, which is a species of market activism more akin to a boycott of the State than to an armed revolution. For example, I make a small amount of money selling art. I work and earn money (minus income tax), which I imagine I own. Then I purchase raw materials (minus sales tax), which I imagine I own. I mix those materials with my time and labor, which I imagine I own. At the end of this process, I imagine that I am the sole proprietor of the resulting product. So, if someone desires, I trade that product to them at some small profit. And the State imagines that it has some claim to that small profit. I already paid taxes on every step in the process except one, my time and labor. Which means the State imagines that I am not the sole proprietor of my time and labor. They think they own me, and I disagree. So, I produce my product without any license, without any regulation, and without any taxes. I think I own myself, so I act like I own myself, and this is my crime.

Whether people conceive of this activity as secessionist in nature, that's precisely what it is. Consent is withdrawn, and the moral legitimacy of the State is questioned one dollar at a time. For many this is a conscious decision, but for considerably more this is born out of necessity. Many Bay Area flea markets now have family-run cash-for-gold exchanges. In San Francisco, increased taxes and regulations have made many restaurants insolvent, and gourmet chefs now serve top-quality food out of rolling carts in the street, using Twitter and Facebook to advertise. Even though city officials have tried to regulate and tax this growing industry, many vendors find the permit process so complicated and expensive that they just don't comply. When a permit to sell the products you own can cost you $10,000, who wouldn't opt for the gray market?

For those inspired by these ideas, step one occurs right now. Right where you're sitting. Before you even finish this article. In your heart of hearts, join the majority of Americans who don't consent, and make the intention to act upon that. Online tools make it virtually free to start. Joining the counter-economy, and beginning your economic independence is as easy as getting paid to do what you love.

# What About the Poor?!

It's time to talk about that old objection: "What about the poor?!" In my mental undulations through libertarianism, that was the hardest objection for me personally to give up. In fact, to this day there is a little Statist in my head who chimes in from time to time. So, for those Statists who think that the best way to help the poor is to elect a class of unaccountable people with a monopoly on violence, who put guns to our heads and fleece our wealth, skim the cream off the top for themselves, and then throw the bones to the poor, I'd like to tell you about Larry Moore. There have been a handful of articles published about Larry, but I'm not sure the State-worshiping journalists at the *San Francisco Chronicle* fully realize just how instructive his story is. So, I humbly submit the following executive summary and commentary.

For six years Larry was a hapless, homeless drunk, living under a bridge, begging for spare change from strangers. In September 2008 Larry acquired his own shoeshine stand, got himself a nice-looking suit, and starting earning $7 a shine. He hasn't touched a drop of alcohol since. It's not a lot of money, not a prestigious job, but anyone who knows Malcolm X's story knows that shoe shining is the bottom of the economy for the entry-level entrepreneur. Larry's business was so successful that the *Chronicle* ran an article about him in March 2009. They called him "the best-dressed shoeshine man in the city." And when they interviewed him, he said, "I used to push a shopping cart in this town. Now I have my own business. I feel blessed every day!" You see, Larry had a plan to save himself. He was squirreling away the money, saving the $600 he needed to rent an apartment.

Well, then some bureaucrat from the Department of Public Works saw the article and sought out Larry to inform him that he needed to purchase a $491 sidewalk vendor permit. Christine Falvey, spokesbureaucrat from Public Works, said the department's contact with Larry was meant to be... educational: "We certainly don't want to hamper anyone's ability to make a living. Our educational efforts are actually meant to support that effort by making our streets an enjoyable place for people to visit." Bollocks! So, Larry, this saint, dutifully attempted to comply with city laws and handed over almost every penny for this permit. Just one problem: Larry didn't have a valid CA driver's license, and had to send away for a replacement birth certificate from Kansas. This bureaucratic SNAFU was described in a second article published on the 4th of June.

The response of the public was described in an article less than a week later: "Hundreds of customers flooded his make-shift stand with shoes and money in hand... After collecting nearly $1,000 from so many new clients, Moore is finally able to pay his way into some temporary housing." Congratulations, Larry!

So, why is this important? Because Larry's story exemplifies perfectly how the State (a monopoly on violence) fails to help the poor, but how the free market (the aggregate of all voluntary economic exchanges) absolutely succeeds. Let me explain.

In the beginning of our story, Larry is a broken man living in a nation with one of the most bloated federal welfare programs in the world, in the most socialist state in the union, in the most lefty pinko city in the state. If a violent monopoly was going to solve poverty anywhere, it would be in San Francisco, and yet Larry slipped through the social safety net for six years. The State did nothing for this man—but generous people did. And if you examine it statistically, you'll see that the more tax money the State takes for the social safety net, the more bureaucratic and inefficient it becomes. So, we know no State solution is ever going to solve the problem of poverty. However, we also know the fair market value of a homeless drunk to well-meaning strangers. This is the true social safety net, and it's a function of the free market, the aggregate of all voluntary economic exchanges. At the very bottom, it is voluntary interaction in the market, not coercive redistribution by the State, that kept Larry fed for six years. Despite estimates of 40–60% taxation in this country, the market is still providing for the poor. So, a coercive tax takes money out of the safety net that works, and puts it into the safety net that doesn't.

And now the little Statist is screaming, "But without the State, the poor will starve in the streets!" And I think that's kind of funny. Is there some reason why you think people who wouldn't give money to the poor would vote for a bureaucrat to take it from them by force? I mean, the fact that Americans continually vote for larger and larger welfare programs seems to imply that helping the poor is a pretty universal value in American society. If it's a universal value, we don't need to be forced to act on it. If it isn't a universal value, then Americans aren't going to vote for it. The very fact that nearly every single person I've ever had this conversation with instantly responds, "What about the poor!" tells me that Americans are mostly good people, and we are able to help the poor without coercion.

Then enters the shoeshine stand. Entrepreneurship is how the free market raises the poor out of the safety net. In a free market, absolutely everyone has value and can create wealth from nothing. With just a minimum of creativity and ambition, anyone can begin earning money for themselves, and no one is worthless. Statism tells us that some people *are* worthless, which is why it usually results in some sort of genocide. By imposing a minimum wage, the centrally planned economy raises the barrier of entry into the market and prevents people like Larry from participating. People in Larry's situation have value, but they are prevented from earning based on that value because they have dropped beneath the minimum. They have to mow lawns, shine shoes, or cover themselves in silver spray paint and put on a street performance. Why? Because these activities still occur in the free market. Were it not for minimum wage laws, Larry would have been allowed to prove his value to an employer by offering to work for a reduced starting wage. He could have swept hair in a barber shop for $4 an hour and earned $600 in less than two months. But no employer is going to risk $8 an hour, and all the taxes and liability that come with employing someone, on a homeless drunk. So, despite the raised barrier to entry preventing the homeless from rising out of poverty, the market is still finding value in the poor who have an entrepreneurial spirit. Coercive minimum wage laws take jobs away from people who can prove their value in the free market and give jobs to bureaucrats who cannot prove their value.

And now the little Statist is screaming, "But without government, greedy capitalists will exploit the workers!" And I think that's kind of funny. Is there some invisible difference between a capitalist and a bureaucrat? We're all human beings, motivated by similar needs, right? OK, then what makes you think that a business owner—who interacts with people on a voluntary basis, must prove the value of their services, and must maintain a positive reputation or risk a boycott—would exploit people more than a bureaucrat, who wields coercive violence, has a monopoly on his services, and is only accountable to the public once in an election cycle? In your experience, are violent people with no competition or liability more virtuous? I mean, the free market boycotts products for exploiting dolphins.

Then enters the State. Can you imagine! The State that supposedly embodies the public desire for charity completely ignores Larry for six years—and then, when they learn of his independent success, they swoop in and take his every penny. Just when he was on the verge of actually lifting himself off the street, he's attacked by the third head of the hydra: licensing laws. The ability of the State to license is the ability of the State to prohibit. If you need to ask for State permission, you don't have a right; you have a privilege. I'm not sure what the reason for the "sidewalk vendor permit" is, but I know why it's important to the Department of Public Works: because everyone—the capitalist, the bureaucrat, the grade school teacher, the celebrity, the poor, you, me, Barack Obama, *everyone*—acts upon market incentives. And the State acquires revenue through licensing laws. Plain and simple. The difference, however, is that the State is not required to prove its value. It is a monopoly on coercive violence, willing to extort $491 from every sidewalk vendor, effectively keeping the poor in poverty.

And now the little Statist is screaming... Nothing. And I think that's kind of funny. Because what's he going to say—"Without the government, poor people will all be selling stuff on the street"? "They'll be providing value in the market, earning wealth, satisfying customers, and improving their condition"? This is always the end result of any rational discussion about coercive violence. Eventually the Statist runs out of arguments from fear or from some vague concept of morality, and has nothing left but irrational prejudice, which is a dangerous motivation when people's lives and prosperity are at stake.

Then enters the free market. Larry was not saved by the State. Larry was saved by the free market. All it took was a little advertising in the form of a newspaper article and there were hundreds of people lined up for blocks to get their shoes shined. Because the free market is not greedy, calculating corporations—the free market is the aggregate of all voluntary economic exchanges. The free market is you, and every economic decision you make every day. And in the free market, in the hearts of people, the homeless have value, the downtrodden have value, charity has value, and Larry has value. All that it takes for good to prevail is for people to live their values without coercion.

So I hope this has been helpful. And I hope you'll go to the corner of New Montgomery and Market Street in San Francisco and get your shoes shined by Larry Moore, the best-dressed shoeshine man in San Francisco.

# A Radical Thought Experiment

Today is Independence Day, or as I call it, Secession Day. So I have a radical thought experiment.

Supreme Court Justice Antonin Scalia made the comment: "If there was any Constitutional issue resolved by the Civil War, it is that there is no right to secede."

Apparently, in some mad fantasy, he imagines the responsibility of interpreting the Constitution doesn't fall on the judicial branch, but instead on the executive branch, in the form of military aggression. Not that it matters. Secessionists don't accept the Constitution, or the Supreme Court's interpretation. If there is no natural right to secession, America owes England some serious reparations.

I have my own mad fantasy. See, I think that the whole concept of America was based on the idea that states were sovereign and free to experiment with different systems of governance to see what worked best. Then this small, practically insignificant central government, with incredibly limited enumerated powers would kind of keep the peace between states. After all, this whole liberty thing was kind of new at the time, and people weren't totally sure it was a good idea. So they wanted a kind of kill switch in place in case it got out of control.

Well... as it turns out, it's the central government that got out of control. Didn't see that coming. Apparently, people are so concerned with controlling the lives of people they hardly know, that they all want the central government to do things it wasn't authorized to do. So it grows and grows and grows until all that liberty stuff is gone, and the whole thing teeters on the verge of economic collapse while going around the world to look for new people's lives to control.

Oops.

I'm of the opinion that New Hampshire solved the laboratory of democracy riddle a long time ago. The smallest government with the lowest taxes is ranked first in quality of life, first for child well-being and has the lowest poverty rate in the Union. Seems clear enough.

So, if the results of the laboratory experiment aren't painfully obvious, let's shake the beakers. Face it, the ideological differences between liberals and conservatives are irreconcilable, and it's unconscionable to subject one to the bad ideas of the other against their will. Public debate is getting us nowhere because both sides are buried in their own propaganda. We need to actually see the tangible results of unfettered liberalism and unfettered conservatism. So, next presidential election, let both candidates win. Let the Republican run the red states and the Democrat run the blue states. Split the

Congress—there're more than enough "representatives" to go around. Let the liberals try to create their socialist welfare utopia without the Republican dime and see what happens. Let the Republicans build their corporatist warfare empire without the Democrat dime and see where it gets them.

Oh, but I think we can do better. Let's let all the separatist movements test their ideas too. Let the Libertarians run an independent Alaska. Let the Green Party run the Vermont Republic. The Lone Star State never really wanted to be part of the Union anyway. But let's get really crazy. Give Hawaii their Kingdom back. Let the Lakota Nation have their sovereignty. Let the Black Panthers have a piece of Louisiana for their Republic of New Afrika. Don't forget the Conch Republic in Key West. And while we're at it, let's let the anarchists have New Hampshire. After all, what's an experiment without a control group?

What's the worst that could happen? After four years, we'll take score. See how everyone did. Then we'll know. We can finally stop arguing hypotheticals and theory, and start working with some real observable consequences.

Here's the thought experiment:

How do you feel right now? I'm sure some of you are pretty excited by this idea. Some of you may even be part of these secession movements and you cheer the notion of a little independence from the federal government. Some, if not most, of you are pretty pissed off at me right now. You're ready to scream that I'm unpatriotic, a bad American, a terrorist, a traitor. For what? Thinking about it?

Secession is as American as it gets, if you think about. Don't forget, this experiment started with secession from England, and they fought a revolution over it. I don't want a bloody revolution. I just want a little freedom. But keep in mind... I didn't invent all these secession movements. Virtually every state has some group that wants out. America is full of unpatriotic bad Americans. Do you really want them in your Union?

Think of it like this: Let's pretend this mad fantasy of mine actually happened. If you're a liberal, imagine if you could have all your free-health-care, environmentalist, peacenik dreams come true without the Republican representatives gumming up the gears of progress. And if you're a conservative, imagine if you could pass all pro-life, pro-gun, anti-immigrant, anti-tax legislation you wanted without the liberal representatives gridlocking the system. Not only would you both get to see all your great ideas actually realized, but be honest: Won't you feel just a little vindicated to see the other guy fail?

After four years of that, do you really think everyone will be eager to sign back up with the federal government? I don't think so. If not, what's holding this house of cards together right now? Is it just some weird obsession with eagles and flags and patriot songs? Do you just like the shape of the map? Why are we holding these people in the Union against their will? When did the Constitution become a suicide pact? If it is something more that holds us together, like all that liberty stuff, isn't it a little hypocritical to deny all these secession movements their own little experiment in independence? At this point in the game, couldn't we use a little radical outside-the-box thinking?

The Declaration of Independence offers an alternative to secession. It reads: "Whenever any Form of Government becomes destructive of these ends [life, liberty, and property], it is the right of the People to alter or to abolish it." If a secessionist movement is untenable, how about an abolitionist movement? Any form of involuntary servitude is, after all, a form of slavery. Rather than pitting the Union states against a new Confederacy, in effect pitting the slaves against each other, why not strike the tree of tyranny at the root? Let's discuss abolishing the federal government altogether.

# The Genesis of the Shire Society

The seeds of a voluntary society have been sown in Lancaster, New Hampshire. Participants in the annual Porcupine Freedom Festival held a signing ceremony to inaugurate their founding document, The Shire Society Declaration, which some have called a new Declaration of Independence.

PorcFest is the annual summer festival of the Free State Project, which is a movement of liberty-loving individuals moving to New Hampshire to consolidate their efforts toward establishing a free society. To date over 10,000 have pledged to move (myself included), and an estimated 1,000 have already relocated there. Many have taken the political route, running for elected offices and organizing in political advocacy groups, but the greater victories have been achieved by those who have adopted the strategy of civil disobedience and non-cooperation. These early movers and New Hampshire natives are proving to be the true champions of liberty activism in America today.

The outside-the-system activism is focused in Keene, New Hampshire, which has been dubbed "the liberty media capital of the world." The genesis of the Shire Society occurred on the local message board FreeKeene.com, where Ian Freeman, host of the nationally syndicated radio show *Free Talk Live* posted:

> If signing declarations and Constitutions hundreds of years ago gave "them" legitimacy, perhaps we should consider doing the same? That way we can claim to have our own society – "see, here's our piece of paper with signatures on it!"

At the signing ceremony, Freeman added:

> "People who work inside the system say things to me like, 'Well you're part of our society and we've got a social contract.' Well, no, I'm not part of your society. I don't want to be part of your society. Your society is a violent one, and societies are supposed to be voluntary by definition."

The Shire Society is a voluntary association of individuals committed to the ideals of peace and liberty. The Shire Society Declaration is intended to announce their non-violent withdrawal of consent from the coercive State society.

Sam Dodson, one of the initial signers, is the host of the Obscured Truth Network, a media company that produces documentaries of interaction with law enforcement and State bureaucracy, exposing the violence, hypocrisy, and ignorance of their own system. At the signing ceremony, Sam described the Shire Society Declaration this way:

> "It's really about acknowledging that man has tried one form of government after another after another, but we've recognized that it's time we evolved past the need for one group of people to force their will, force their ideas, and force their solutions on everybody else by using coercion and violence."

He goes on:

> "Anybody can read this and understand it. It's not geographically bound. It's just a personal choice that people make. Basically, by signing, they are affirming their commitment to a voluntary society. To work towards that. To move towards that. To stay in that state of mind."

I had the honor of hand-writing the Shire Society Declaration, which was done with a classic dip pen on large hemp paper. As the artist, I had the unique privilege of being the first to place my name on this historic document amongst the now hundreds of liberty luminaries who have signed.

# Artist's Statement

Legend records that when delegates gathered in Philadelphia to sign the Declaration of Independence, their courage wavered. Signing would be an act of treason under British law, and no one wished to be the first. From the back of the room, a stranger stood and delivered an oration that galvanized their courage. This became known as "The Speech of the Unknown."

Now a new crop of delegates gathers in New Hampshire. Though they may not fear the scaffold, they understand that the behemoth created that day in Philadelphia has grown larger and more intrusive than the British crown could have ever dreamed of being.

And if your courage wavers, consider this: These words will not only reach the tyrants, who have trampled on mankind long enough. They will speak to those trodden beneath the tyrant's boot. They will say to a persecuted world, "Behold! The rituals of the old world are dead, and you stand on the threshold of Liberty." So, if your heart bears witness to the truth of it, then shake the shackles of the world and sign.

I'm truly honored to put my name on this parchment. I have no doubt that history is being made today, and I am grateful to contribute a relic to that legacy. One day, God willing, I will join you in the Free State.

# The Shire Society Declaration

WE, THE UNDERSIGNED witnesses to the lesson of history—that no form of political governance may be relied upon to secure the individual rights of life, liberty, or property—now therefore establish and provide certain fundamental precepts measuring our conduct toward one another, and toward others:

FIRST, each individual is the exclusive proprietor of his or her own existence and all products thereof, holding no obligations except those created by consent;

SECOND, no individual or association of individuals, however constituted, has the right to initiate force against any other individual;

THIRD, each individual has the inalienable right of self-defense against the initiation of force;

FOURTH, explicit voluntary association is the only means by which binding obligations may be created, and claims based on association or relationships to which any party did not consent are empty and invalid;

FIFTH, rights are neither collective nor additive in character, and no group can possess rights in excess of those belonging to its individual members;

We hereby declare our commitment to peace, individual sovereignty, and independence, and join the Shire Society.

# Chapter Six: Police State

## What Does a Police State Look Like?

In George Orwell's dystopian classic *1984*, the protagonist, Winston Smith, indulges in one of the most heinous of clandestine crimes against the Party: He keeps a diary. He is immediately drowned in a flood of emotion. His long-repressed hatred for the Party bursts in ink as he scrawls over and over, "Down with Big Brother. Down with Big Brother! DOWN WITH BIG BROTHER!" When his judgment returns, fear seizes him, not only because he has committed the crime, but because he has thought the crime. In Winston Smith's world, The Party seeks to control not only the actions of people, but their very thoughts.

You know we live in an Orwellian nightmare when a prize for peace is awarded to a man of war. As one reads the ignoble remarks of Obama during his acceptance of the Nobel Peace Prize, one can hardly keep from hearing the doublespeak slogans of The Party.

When Barack tells us that "instruments of war have a role to play in preserving the peace," and that our troops are not makers of war but "wagers of peace," I hear Big Brother saying "WAR IS PEACE."

When Barack tells us that US military occupation around the world does not exist to "impose our will," but to ensure that the rest of the world can "live in freedom and prosperity," I hear Big Brother saying "FREEDOM IS SLAVERY."

When Barack tells us that there is "little scientific dispute" that climate change is a security issue, and that it's not only a topic for scientists, but for "military leaders," I hear Big Brother saying "IGNORANCE IS STRENGTH."

Indeed, in America we are still free to keep a diary. We can even publish it on the Internet. But what George Orwell was saying in *1984* was that it's not enough for a police state to control the actions of the people. To succeed, totalitarianism must control the *minds* of the people. It must criminalize thought itself.

I believe America has begun to do just that. It was never debated in Congress. The bill was never signed into law. The public was never informed. But the institution of thoughtcrime already exists like a cage enclosing the minds of most Americans. If I am wrong, you will have no objection to indulging in a little thoughtcrime with me. But if I'm right, you will feel the same apprehension Winston Smith felt writing in his diary, and then maybe you will see the bars as clearly as I do.

When most Americans imagine a police state, they recall the rise and fall of German fascism. Goosestepping storm troopers and Gestapo police demanding to see papers. They think of government surveillance, secret police, and extrajudicial death squads. Most Americans also connect these images with phrases like "It could never happen here" and "America is the land of the free." Police don riot gear and launch tear gas and flash grenades at non-violent civilians, and people think, "It's an isolated incident." Federal agents monitor phone calls and emails, track vehicles with global positioning systems, and interrogate people on the flimsiest of pretexts, and people think, "I have nothing to hide." SWAT teams with military equipment conduct no-knock raids into private homes based on anonymous tips, and people think, "It won't happen to me. I'm a law-abiding citizen."

These mantras are the bars of the cage. They quiet the mind, reduce anxiety, and promote a docile attitude. They prevent the people from seeing the cage. But how bad does it have to get before the mantras stop working? Because questioning that foundational premise of American society, that we are free, is precisely the thoughtcrime that I intend to commit. So, I want you to push the bars aside and sincerely ask yourself a very important question: "What does a police state look like?"

No, really! Think about it.

Do you have a picture in your mind?

OK... now I want to tell you about the land of the free.

First, I want to tell you about 4-year-old Abigail Krutsinger. One weekend she set up a quaint little lemonade stand in Coralville, Iowa, serving ice-cold lemonade to passersby for 25 cents a glass. After just 30 minutes, police came and shut down the operation. The officer told her mother, "This isn't the first time I've had to do this." Apparently police had shut down at least three other lemonade stands that weekend. The reason? They didn't have the proper permits. Coralville City Administrator Kelly Hayworth said the crackdown was to "stay in step [Or is it "lockstep"?] with the county health department."

I already know what you're thinking: "It's an isolated incident." Well, not really. Lydia Coenen was selling lemonade in her front yard in Appleton, Wisconsin, which had been a summer tradition for six years. Then police came and shut her down. Her father asked if they could make an exception. They said they "had to follow orders..." I mean, "...ordinance." Three boys in Bethesda, Maryland, were selling lemonade to raise money for children's cancer research. Same story. Cops shut them down and hit their parents with a $500 ticket for vending without having the proper permits.

Similar lemonade crackdowns have happened in McAllen, Texas; Midway, Georgia; Portland, Oregon; Tulare, California; New York City; San Francisco; Philadelphia... The list goes on. And it doubles if you include busted Girl Scout cookie vendors.

Feeling apprehensive yet? That's enough for me. When jackbooted thugs, blindly following stupid orders, patrol residential streets demanding to see the papers of children so the city gets their cut, I call it a police state. But I know a lot of you are unconvinced. So, let's move on.

Let me tell you about Steven Anderson. He's a Baptist preacher who was Tasered, beaten, and brutalized by Arizona border patrol officers. In the words of George Orwell, "If you want a picture of the future, imagine a boot stamping on a human face, forever." That future was realized in this case. After two officers smashed the windows of his car with hammers, hit him with Tasers, and dragged him out of his vehicle bloody and paralyzed, they smashed his face into the glass with their boot. What was his offense? He asked to know what reasonable suspicion they had to search his vehicle without a warrant. After admitting they had nothing, they called him a terrorist and proceeded, unhindered by law or conscience.

Not sure what the mantra is for this one... "Just a couple bad apples" is probably the best we've got. Or maybe you're an anti-immigration zealot and consider locking down the border to be a really important counter-terrorism measure. Here's the catch: Steven Anderson was born and raised in America, and this took place fifty miles from Mexico, at an internal immigration checkpoint, not actually on the border.

A strip of America a hundred miles in from every border and coastline is now what the ACLU calls "the Constitution-Free Zone," which means we're going to start seeing checkpoints all over the place, and we're going to start seeing "bad apples" like this all the time. A similar incident occurred in Michigan to Canadian sci-fi author Peter Watts, who, when trying to leave the United States, asked the same question: Why? He was punched in the face, pepper-sprayed, handcuffed, jailed overnight without legal representation, and finally dumped into the Canadian winter without his coat and less one laptop computer.

A distinguishing characteristic of a police state is that officers act with impunity. If they accuse you of "terrorism," all bets are off. Read any news story about police misconduct and the most the department ever says is that it is in the process of an investigation—and even when individual officers are found to be in error, they are "punished" with a paid vacation. Police officers are unaccountable for their actions. So as the police force grows, both in number and in arms, brutality like this is going to become more common.

Are you feeling apprehensive yet?

Let me tell you about Kelly Thomas. He was a homeless man who was Tasered repeatedly, brutally beaten, and ultimately killed by six police officers in Fullerton, California. Eyewitnesses say that the six officers had him hogtied on his belly as they stood over him beating him with the butts of their guns and kicking him. In his final moments of life he was heard crying out for his father as they beat him into unconsciousness and beyond. He had no weapon and was a 135-pound weakling lorded over by six heavily armed officers. But they said he was resisting arrest, so all bets are off. Resistance equals death, obviously. Multiple videos have been released of the incident. I'm almost grateful they can't be shared in print.

Not sure what the mantra is for this one... Nothing is more indicative of a police state than the impunity with which American police officers act today. In stories like these, the internal investigation is always hindered by the code of silence that officers afford one another. Is there anyone left who will not admit that this is a police state? Just try saying it out loud: "Police state." See how the words feel in your mouth. You can whisper it if you are afraid.

Let me tell you about Kenneth Wright. A SWAT team raided his Stockton, California, home at 6 AM, grabbing him by the neck, kneeing his back, dragging him out in his boxers, and locking him and his three children, 3, 7, and 11, in a police cruiser for six hours while his house was tossed. Funny thing, Wright wasn't the one they were looking for. They were actually executing a warrant issued by the Department of Education for his estranged wife, who didn't live there. It was originally reported that the warrant was issued because of her defaulted student loans. The press secretary of the Department of Education later denied this, but said that because it was an "ongoing criminal investigation," the DOE couldn't give any specifics. What he didn't deny was that the Department of Education has the authority to order paramilitary-style dawn raids when investigating crimes like bribery, fraud, and embezzlement of federal student aid funds.

These days no-knock raids are practically routine. Whether it's a SWAT team sent into a nursing home for disabled residents looking for a registered medical marijuana caregiver, or the FDA calling a hit on Amish farmers for selling organic raw milk to appreciative customers, the militarization of the police has touched virtually every community in this country.

Maybe you're saying to yourself, "Why should I worry? I'm a law-abiding citizen." OK. Keep your mantra. Let's move on...

Meet 11-year-old Jon Shiflett. Poor little Jon fell and bumped his head playing in the front yard. Luckily his loving mother whisked him up and applied ice to the bruise, and he was fine. But some busybody neighbor called the paramedics. Paramedics arrived, and recommended a medical examination at the hospital. Jon's father declined—after all, an ambulance ride isn't free. Paramedics left, but reported the incident to social services.

The next day a SWAT team was sent to abduct the boy and bring him to the hospital. They broke through the door and held the entire family at gunpoint while they tore apart the home. In a letter to World Net Daily, Jon's mother writes, "During the attack, one [officer] grabbed my daughter Beth (18 years), who also had a gun to her face, slammed her down and kneed her in the back and held her in that position... My sons Adam (14) and Noah (only 7) lay down willingly, yet they were still forced to put their hands behind their backs and were yelled at to keep their heads down. My daughter Jeanette was coming out from the back bedroom when she was grabbed, drug down the hallway, across a couch and slammed to the ground. The officers then began throwing scissors and screwdrivers across the room (out of our reach, I suppose) and going through our cupboards. I asked if I could make a phone call and was told, 'no.' My daughter asked if that wasn't one of our rights. The reply was made, 'That's only in the movies.'"

The sheriff took Jon, without his parents' consent, to the hospital to get a medical examination. Doctors said it was a light bump, and the family should apply ice to the bruise.

They were also "law-abiding citizens."

Finally, I want to tell you about Private First Class Damien M. Corsetti. His colleagues nicknamed him "the King of Torture," and he was a guard at the lesser-known internment facility at the Bagram Airbase in Afghanistan. Considered by many to be worse than Guantanamo or Abu Ghraib, Bagram has been in use longer, and held more detainees than either. An internal army investigation was held, the details of which were leaked to *The New York Times*. During a military tribunal, witness testimony was given regarding a Saudi detainee whom Corsetti threatened with rape if he did not cooperate. Corsetti pushed his penis in the detainee's face and told him, "This is your god." Corsetti was cleared of all charges because, as his attorney argued, the rules of detainee treatment were unclear to him. The investigation uncovered incidents of brutal beatings, anal rape with sharp objects, and genital abuse.

Similar reports persist to this day, and yet we are supposed to believe that the US military is trying to keep the world free and prosperous? I know those of you on the right are repeating your last mantra, "Everything changed on 9/11!" OK, maybe that's true—but changed into what? Those of you on the left have your mantras too: "But Obama promised to close Guantanamo and outlaw torture!" Never mind that he's yet to make good on that promise, and he's authorized the indefinite detention and assassination of US citizens. You can keep your mantras.

With the constant flow of military veterans into the domestic police force, you can bet more and more of these monsters will be raiding homes, guarding checkpoints, and demanding papers in your neighborhood. Remember that totalitarianism was not the aim of the Nazi Party. They were National Socialists. The tyrannical government was just the inevitable result of the collusion between corporations, government, and military. Doesn't that sound like America? What attribute characterizes a police state that we do not already exhibit? How bad does it have to get before you admit it to yourself... perhaps quietly... in a diary?

# One of These Things Is Not Like the Others

If, like me, you grew up watching *Sesame Street*, you're probably familiar with the "One of these things is not like the others" game. Grover or Oscar or some other Muppet would show the viewers a group of items and ask them to identify the item that didn't belong. Well, I'd like to play that game with some stories I've read in the news.

First, let me tell you about Faiz Khalaf. He lived and worked on a family farm north of Baghdad with his young wife, his three children (aged 5, 3, and 5 months), his 74-year-old mother, his sister, and his two nieces (aged 5 and 3). In 2006, US forces stormed his home in a pre-dawn raid. Shots were fired and the entire Khalaf family was killed. At the time, local police, neighbors, and multiple reporters called this a mass execution of innocent civilians. Multiple Iraqi TV stations aired gruesome footage of the children's bodies (winning hearts and minds!). Angered Iraqi officials demanded some kind of action be taken, but US officials denied that anything inappropriate occurred. A US internal investigation cleared the US troops of all wrongdoing, claiming that at least one insurgent had been seized during the battle. A US diplomatic cable made public by WikiLeaks suggested a different story. The cable made no reference to the arrest of any suspect, or resistance from any residents. Autopsies performed showed that every member of the Khalaf family had been handcuffed and shot in the head. After they were all dead, US troops called for an air strike on the home, burned three vehicles, and killed their livestock in an apparent effort to destroy evidence. Philip Alston, a high-ranking United Nations investigator, reported that executions like this "were hardly an isolated incident."

Second, let me tell you about LaShanda Smith. She's suing Chicago Public Schools because her son was one of several first-graders at Carver Primary School who were "disciplined" for talking in class by being handcuffed and detained for hours without being allowed to contact their parents. The arresting officer removed the youngsters from class in cuffs, held them in an isolated room away from any other adults, and told them that "they were going to prison and would never see their parents again." In her lawsuit filed in Cook County Circuit Court, Smith says that her son "sustained injuries of a permanent, personal and pecuniary nature." *Pecuniary* means, "of or relating to money." Don't feel bad—I had to look it up. It sounds to me like she's better off home-schooling anyway. Their family attorney said the Chicago Board of Education ignored repeated attempts to resolve the matter outside of court, and no disciplinary action against the officer has been reported. No surprise.

Finally, let me tell you about Derek Lopez. He's a 14-year-old boy who got into a fight at a school bus stop. He reportedly punched the other boy once. This was witnessed by police officer Daniel Alvarado, who decided to intervene. Alvarado had been reprimanded sixteen times in the previous four years, specifically for insubordination and failure to follow supervisors' directives. So, the cop ordered Derek to "freeze," but instead the boy ran and disappeared into the neighborhood across the street from the high school. Alvarado called dispatch and his supervisor directed him to stay at the bus stop with the other boy and not to go searching the neighborhood. So, of course he followed orders.... Just kidding. He sped into the neighborhood. Derek jumped over a fence and hid in a shed in the back yard of a house. Alvarado exited the patrol car, weapon drawn, and stormed through the gate into the yard. Within seconds Alvarado shot the unarmed boy hiding in the shed. The homeowner, who was an EMT, called 911. Derek died from his wound in the ambulance 50 minutes later. Rather than terminating Alvarado, the district transferred him to patrol.

So, which of these things is not like the others? Is it Khalaf, because he was in Iraq, while the other two were in the United States? Or is it Smith, because he survived while the other two were killed? Maybe it's Lopez, because the other two were handcuffed and he at least had a decent chance to run and hide? Well, the fact is... I'm pulling your leg a little bit. There is no answer. All three of these stories are tragic expressions of the same systemic problem. When individuals are granted the insignia of authority, the tools of violence, and immunity from accountability, they misbehave. Psychologically speaking, in order for an individual to consign his body over to the military, occupy a foreign land, and attempt to annihilate an evasive enemy, he must dehumanize that enemy and every suspected enemy. That's the only way a team of allegedly sane men and women can enter a home, gather a family in one room, and systematically execute them. They must on some level regard those victims as less than human.

So what happens when those individuals come home?

The militarization of the civilian police force in America is undeniable. Many of those soldiers are swept into a domestic law enforcement position when they should probably be spending some time in a mental health facility. Across the country, local police departments have inherited millions of pieces of surplus military equipment. Military-grade semi-automatic weapons, armored vehicles, helicopters, and other heavy equipment intended for the battlefield are now being used here against us. Tactics and training that was developed for soldiers against foreign insurgents are now implemented by domestic officers against political protesters.

Paramilitary SWAT raids originally meant for violent emergency situations are now routinely used to carry out warrants.

The uncomfortable reality is that the average American civilian is more similar to Faiz Khalaf than to their own domestic "peace officers." Similarly, Daniel Alvarado and other average American cops are more psychologically similar to US soldiers than they are to their own neighbors. Like soldiers, they must dehumanize the criminal and every suspected criminal. They must on some level regard us as less than human. That's the only way they could treat us like livestock.

# Unmanned Aerial Vehicles:
# Coming Soon to Anytown, USA

There's a collection of stories that don't appear connected at first glance—but once we put the pieces together, I think you'll get it. Brace yourself. This is going to be a little rough.

Let's start with Anwar al-Awlaki, the US-born American imam who was killed by a CIA drone in Yemen on September 30, 2011. Al-Awlaki was never charged and received no trial, not even in absentia. He's also not accused of any actual violence, but of allegedly inciting violence as a "spiritual advisor" by emails to the Underwear Bomber, the Fort Hood Shooter, and some others. His principal crime, however you look at it, is speech.

Some important milestones were crossed in this case. First, the President now authorizes the assassination of US citizens. And the order was carried out by the CIA, not the US military, which is subject to far less scrutiny. Second, another US citizen, *Inspire* magazine editor Samir Khan, was also killed, though he was not on the "kill or capture list."

The legal process by which this decision was made has still not been disclosed, despite a Freedom of Information Act request from the ACLU. When asked whether al-Awlaki had received whatever due process he was entitled to, House Intelligence Committee Chairman Mike Rogers said that this case involved "special circumstances" because al-Awlaki was "an enemy combatant by any standard" —except, of course... combat.

The government expects us to accept this because al-Awlaki is a "terrorist"; but that same government is constantly blurring the definition of that word. The FBI called monetary architect Bernard von NotHaus a domestic terrorist for minting silver rounds. House Committee on Homeland Security Chairman Peter King wanted WikiLeaks classified as a terrorist organization. Orlando Mayor Buddy Dyer called the Food Not Bombs organization "food terrorists."

In an opinion piece for the *New York Daily News*, Ron Paul wrote:

> We now have an accepted practice of the president assassinating who he thinks are bad guys... Under our Constitution, American citizens, even those living abroad, must be charged with a crime before being sentenced... What I would not do as President is what Obama has done and continues to do in spectacular fashion: circumvent the rule of law.

But we're just getting started.

The Army contracted several tech firms to design new drone-mounted surveillance equipment. Progeny Systems Corporation has developed algorithms for the military that construct a 3D model of a target's face using aerial photos. Combined with facial recognition software, they expect to be able to tag and track targets from 750 feet in the air. Of course, if the trend of military equipment trickling down to local police departments continues as it has, I'm sure your DMV photo will work just fine.

Charles River Analytics is developing a drone-mounted "Adversary Behavior Acquisition, Collection, Understanding and Summarization" (ABACUS) tool that is designed to spot "adversarial intent" from the air. The system purports to be able to integrate drone footage with other intelligence to apply a "human behavior modeling and simulation engine" to provide "intent-based threat assessments of individuals and groups." In other words, Predator drones will soon be able to determine whether or not you harbor ill will toward the government... or at least provide the pretense for them to claim you do.

Feeling nervous yet? It gets worse.

Ogden, Utah, plans to launch the nation's first domestic surveillance blimp by Christmas 2012. The blimp will be equipped with day- and night-vision cameras, and operated by remote control. The "unmanned aerial vehicles," as Mayor Matthew Godfrey wants to call them, would run for five to seven hours at an altitude of around 400 feet (Well within the 750-foot range of the new military drone equipment). The blimp can follow a pre-programmed route, or be redirected to track an individual or vehicle. Ogden Police Chief Jon Greiner added, "Nobody else in the nation is trying to do this, so the Federal Aviation Administration has no regulations for it." I predict these will soon be common to most metropolitan areas. They reportedly cost less than half the price of a fully loaded patrol car.

Now let's bring all the pieces together:

1) Drone strikes against US citizens branded "terrorists" are OK.

2) Collateral damage of US citizens during drone strikes is OK.

3) The definition of combatant has drifted to include inciteful speech.

4) The definition of terrorist has drifted to include crimes of dissent.

5) Drones are being programmed to detect dissent.

6) Domestic police will soon be using unmanned aerial vehicles.

7) Military technology trickles down to local law

enforcement.

Are you seeing the pattern yet? These puzzle pieces are just waiting for some authoritarian sociopath to fit together. If it's not Obama, or whoever replaces him, it will be some faceless, nameless bureaucrat, or some committee behind closed doors. One by one the precedents will be set. Step by step the policies will change and the contracts will be signed. It is the inevitable nature of government to grow, to push the limits of its power, and to cross new milestones in the transgression of justice.

So... how long will it be before the first Predator drones are flying over Anytown, USA?

# Predator Drones Patrol US Skies Searching for Stray Cows... No Joke

Sometimes it sucks to be right. One of the exciting things about libertarians is how often their predictions come true. Whether it's the ever-increasing price of gold, the collapse of various economic bubbles, or the rise of the police state, it often seems the unofficial slogan of libertarianism is "I told you so." Well, now it's my turn. Two months after I predicted Predator drones would be flying over Anytown, USA, the story broke that a little-known provision in the 2005 immigration bill authorized the use of Predator drones along the US border and allowed other agencies to borrow the drones for "interior law enforcement support." People called me paranoid, but now the same MQ-9 "hunter/killer" drones used for CIA assassinations in Yemen and Pakistan are being used to track down stray cattle in North Dakota... no joke.

They claim the Predator drones used in American skies are for "surveillance and situational awareness only," and are unarmed, at least for now. But that's about as comforting as a sniper in balcony seating saying his rifle is unloaded and he's just using the scope to get a better view of the speaker.

Terrorism is the excuse, as always. In this case, six stray cows wandered onto the 3,000-acre property of the Brossart family. Nelson County Sheriff Kelly Janke went looking for the missing cattle, and three men ordered him off their property, allegedly carrying rifles, which Janke called "brandishing," as they will. But the Brossart family are supposedly members of the Sovereign Citizens movement, which the FBI considers "domestic extremists"—so of course recovering $6,000 worth of beef required a military-grade response. Janke called in reinforcements from Highway Patrol, a bomb squad, a SWAT team, deputy sheriffs from three other counties, and of course, a Predator drone.

The drone returned from the US–Canada border and circled two miles above the family farm, too high to be seen or heard. Meanwhile Janke monitored a live high-resolution feed on his office computer using a password-protected government website called Big Pipe. Once Janke, using thermal imaging, could see that all the suspects were unarmed, he signaled his small army to move in, making the first known arrests of civilians on American soil with the assistance of a Predator drone.

Rodney Brossart, his wife Susan, his daughter Abby, and his three sons Thomas, Jacob, and Alex, face a total of eleven felony charges, mostly related to weapons found in their home. They have all been released on bail, however—so they must not be too dangerous. Don't worry, the six missing cows were recovered. Rodney was apparently under the impression the cows were unclaimed. Just a misunderstanding of open-range law.

Since June, Nelson County police have used Predator drones at least two dozen times. Officials say the FBI and DEA also use Predators in domestic investigations. Michael C. Kostelnik, a retired Air Force general who heads the office that supervises the drones, said Predators are flown "in many areas around the country, not only for federal operators, but also for state and local law enforcement." So it was actually going on long before I even asked the question. Who's paranoid now?

If they call on drones to recover six cows, do you seriously think there isn't a Predator drone flying over every city with an Occupy encampment? And if police can tell when a handful of rural gun-polishers are armed using a thermal camera two miles in the air, why does the TSA have to cup our junk and bombard us with radiation?

# Insect-Sized Micro-Drones

There was a time when claiming that the government was developing surveillance programs to spy on us from the sky was disregarded as the paranoid ramblings of an insane person. The bar has moved, because black helicopters just don't seem that crazy anymore. If you combine the robotic aircraft of *Brave New World* with the surveillance state of *1984*, you pretty much get current US policy.

In February 2012 a House–Senate conference report called for acceleration of the use of "civilian unmanned aerial systems." Notice the name change? Over foreign soil they have the ominous name "Predator drones," but over US soil they change to the more benign-sounding "civilian systems" even though we are talking about the exact same MQ-9 "hunter/killer" drones that the Obama Administration has used hundreds of times to attack civilians in foreign countries. The bill asks for a plan for "the safe integration of civil unmanned aircraft systems into the national airspace system as soon as practicable, but not later than September 30, 2015." The bill also calls for the establishment of test ranges for the drones in cooperation with the Department of Defense. These same provisions already passed in the 2012 National Defense Authorization Act (section 1097), which mandates the establishment of "a program to integrate unmanned aircraft systems into the national airspace system at six test ranges." I'm not sure what they're testing exactly. It seems to me they have already been pretty well tested in the field.

While that's been going on in Congress, the Defense Advanced Research Projects Agency (DARPA) has been funding research for the next generation of unmanned aerial drones. Soon a swarm of insect-sized "Micro Aerial Vehicles" (MAVs) will be on their way. Up until now re-creating insect flight has been notoriously difficult for mechanical engineers, but thanks to two DARPA research projects, it may be closer than ever.

Tiras Lin, an engineering undergrad at Johns Hopkins University, had the bright idea of taking a super high-speed video camera down to the entomology department to capture a butterfly in flight. What he discovered was that the maneuverability of a butterfly has more to do with shifting its body mass to modify its inertia than with flapping its wings. This discovery means the development of new mechanical micro-drones able to navigate urban environments, where variable weather conditions and complex obstacles made them impossible before.

When the US military wants to play God, they outsource their research facilities to Israel. In Haifa there's an unusual aeronautics laboratory full of terrariums swarming with flies, grasshoppers, beetles, dragonflies, and bees. A team of scientists, funded by the US military, are conducting experiments designed to remotely control the flight of living insects. Having trouble reverse engineering the flight of insects in robotics? No problem. Just hijack 300 million years of evolution.

Electrodes are inserted into each muscle group of the insects to record the electrical signals of every minuscule movement. Then the insects are placed in a flight simulator, which is essentially a wind tunnel. The electrical signals in the insect's muscles are recorded and translated into an editable code, and then new electrical signals are sent into the insect, triggering new movements. Researchers have already gained control of the insects when they are connected to the simulator. Now it's just a matter of figuring out the remote controls.

Soon drones won't just be the robot eye watching us from above, they'll be the bug buzzing around our face, and when the swarm of micro-drones comes, they may be indistinguishable from actual bugs, because they will *be* actual bugs.

Imagine a swarm of video-capable micro-drones blowing through a public demonstration and capturing a mug shot of every participant. With a high enough resolution camera they could collect retina scans of virtually everyone. Or how about a mosquito drone equipped to capture DNA samples without anyone even knowing? Forget checking for a bulky GPS tracker under your car. Take a second look at the critter caught in your windshield wiper. How long before these things are weaponized to deliver a little dose of arsenic, or perhaps some organic compound that would alert less suspicion? Does it still sound like the paranoid ramblings of a conspiracy theorist? Because I think it's just a matter of time.

# While You Were Sleeping

There was a time in my life when I used to love wild conspiracy theories about the growth of a totalitarian police state. I used to claim, with tongue in cheek, that Arnold Schwarzenegger was chosen as a candidate for Governor of California because his appearance as a reprogrammed benevolent cyborg in *Terminator 3*, just weeks before his campaign, would soften the public's objections to voting machines. Or, that Starbucks Coffee, with its numerous references to sirens and lotus-eaters of Greek mythology, must surely contain some neurological toxin designed to pacify the masses for the global elite. But now it's hard to imagine anything the State wouldn't do to trample the few remaining liberties that are left uninfringed. At best the US Constitution appears to have taught the tyrants to be more creative in their subterfuge. Ten years ago 9/11 provided the pretext for the Patriot Act, which was openly criticized and widely protested for years. Yet by today's standards the Patriot Act seems quaint. These days the tyrannical laws roll out so fast I hardly have time to write about one before the next half dozen come along. But while this is happening, most of the country is oblivious.

While you were sleeping, Congress drove the final nail in the coffin of freedom of speech by voting 388-to-3 in favor of making it a federal offense to protest government. A provision in HR 347 (a.k.a. the "Trespass Bill") was presented as making protests at the White House illegal, but it actually criminalized protests anywhere the Secret Service or any person under their protection is located, whether you know they are there or not. Currently that means the President, former Presidents, their families, Presidential and Vice Presidential candidates, foreign heads of state, and a number of miscellaneous US officials. In other words, it's now a federal crime to heckle Joe Biden, or engage in any kind of political protest at presidential debates, Democratic or Republican National Conventions, G8 and NATO summits, and potentially even Super Bowls. But here's the kicker: They don't actually have to inform you where these free speech-free zones are. And don't be surprised if the next move is expanding the list of bureaucrats who enjoy the special status of Secret Service protection.

While you were sleeping, Attorney General Eric Holder announced that the US military can execute American citizens without trial because "'due process' and 'judicial process' are not one and the same." So basically the Constitutional guarantee of "due process" is not a right to a fair trial, as it's been understood since its inception. It's simply a right to some process of some kind to be determined by the sociopath calling the hit. Holder did not explain how "due process" is ensured without "judicial process." I guess they'll simply assume anyone accused of terrorism is guilty, declare their capture "unfeasible," and *Presto!* Who needs a judicial branch? Of course, when FBI Director Robert Mueller was asked by Representative Tom Graves from Georgia if this executive power only applies to US citizens overseas or also to those at home, he said, "Uh, I'm not certain whether that was addressed or not." In other words, it's just a matter of time.

While you were sleeping, Congress mandated that all new cars be equipped with data-recording "black boxes" just like aircraft. Senate Bill 1813 has been dubbed the "Moving Ahead for Progress in the 21st Century Act" or the "MAP-21 Act."

It requires "Mandatory Event Data Recorders" to be installed in all new cars starting in 2015. No discussion. No debate. And most important, no deference to a Supreme Court decision made just three months before. The highest court in the land ruled that planting recording devices on our cars violates the Fourth Amendment and requires a warrant from a judge—and next thing you know, Congress is mandating that they be put on every car on the road. Why let the Constitution stand in the way of the relentless march of petty tyrants and bureaucrats? Can we just stop pretending that the Bill of Rights means anything to these thugs?

While you were sleeping, a former NSA official came forward with details on a heavily fortified data center that is being constructed in Bluffdale, Utah, that should be up and running in September 2013. When completed, it will encompass 1 million square feet and will include four facilities filled with rows and rows of computer servers. The Spy Center will be secretly capturing, storing, deciphering, and analyzing vast amounts of data transmitted through the world's telecommunications networks, including private emails, phone calls, travel itineraries, financial information, foreign diplomatic secrets, walkie-talkie frequencies, and browsing histories. It's being called "total information awareness." The finished Spy Center will be the information hub of a vast surveillance complex that's been under construction for over a decade, granting them warrantless access to just about every piece of private data.

Are you awake yet? Can it be any more obvious? When Obama approved the National Defense Authorization Act, he essentially suspended habeas corpus. Now they are laying the legal groundwork to impose the death penalty on US citizens without a trial, while simultaneously creating the infrastructure to carry out the executions from the sky. So, go out and protest—if you dare.

# Chapter Seven: The Candid World

## The South Park Muhammad Cartoon

> And do not insult those whom they call upon instead of God, lest they insult God out of spite in their ignorance. We have made the deeds of each people fair seeming to themselves, and to their Lord is their return, and He will inform them of what they used to do. (Quran 6:108)

I've been thinking about this *South Park* controversy, and there are numerous approaches I'd like to take. It seems as if most American Muslims just rolled their eyes and went on with their lives, with the exception of one particularly obnoxious group in New York. We'll get to that, but first some background information:

When *South Park* celebrated its 200th episode with a parade of inside jokes, those of us who don't watch the show regularly were largely lost. The setup was a natural for the series: the small mountain town faces a class action lawsuit from every celebrity they have ever offended, which will end in certain ruin unless they can meet the demands of Tom Cruise to deliver to him the Prophet Muhammad.

Cruise, and the other celebrities, hope to steal Muhammad's magical protection from ridicule. The remainder of the episode is spent trying to figure out how to deliver Muhammad to the celebrities without showing him to the audience and thereby incurring the wrath of Muslim extremists. At first he is kept in a U-Haul truck, and then brought out obscured in a giant bear suit. (I suspect this was a reference to the incident where a British school teacher was arrested in Sudan and charged with blasphemy for allowing her class to democratically name a class teddy bear "Muhammad.") But in the end, it's not the Muslim extremists who detonate a car bomb, it's the Gingers, people with red hair, freckles, and pale skin, who have faced ridicule in *South Park*'s past.

Following the episode, a New York–based group called "Revolution Muslim" published a veiled threat against *South Park* creators Trey Parker and Matt Stone. In full disclosure, their website was shut down before I actually saw it, but they reportedly published grotesque photos of Theo van Gogh, who was killed by Muslim extremists in 2004. Revolution Muslim implied that the *South Park* creators could meet a similar fate. They also posted the addresses of the headquarters of Comedy Central in New York and the *South Park* production company in Los Angeles. Other than Revolution Muslim, I haven't seen any outrage from Muslims about this episode. In fact, most of the Muslim response seems tame. Zahed Amanullah, writing for the Guardian.co.uk regards the Revolution Muslim duo as "a couple of misfits," and says the *South Park* episode is just not an issue for most Muslims. Ahmed Rehab, writing for the *Chicago Tribune*, regards Revolution Muslim as "radical goons," and calls the whole controversy contrived. Wajahat Ali, the playwright best known for *The Domestic Crusaders*, satirized the entire controversy with a short skit about South Park's neighboring town, East Park, where a radical group called "De-volution Islam" stands alone amongst the majority who understand that art is used to promote discussion.

While Parker and Stone insisted that they stood behind their work, Comedy Central caved to the threats by censoring the follow-up 201st episode, in which the story continued. Every mention of Muhammad's name was bleeped, and his image was covered by a big black "CENSORED" box. The episode was utterly incomprehensible unless you already knew what was going on. Many people initially thought the censorship was part of the gag, but according to a statement from Stone and Parker, "It wasn't some meta-joke on our part. Comedy Central added the bleeps. In fact, Kyle's customary final speech was about intimidation and fear. It didn't mention Muhammad at all but it got bleeped too." Both episodes were pulled from the Comedy Central website, but are still widely available on the Internet.

Americans have responded to this in many ways, from hacking the Revolution Muslim website, to chastising Comedy Central for their decision to self-censor. On CNN, Anderson Cooper interviewed Ayaan Hirsi Ali, author of the memoir *Infidel* and the screenplay for Theo van Gogh's movie *Submission*, who is not exactly regarded as an unbiased expert on Islam. In the interview she said, "Growing up as a Muslim I learned that you don't criticize Allah, the Quran or the Prophet Muhammad. And you should participate in condemning and eventually killing anybody who does. That's just what the religion tells us." I don't know what book she's reading, but apparently most of us missed the memo. On *The Daily Show*, Jon Stewart focused on the hypocrisy of Revolution Muslim hiding behind the First Amendment to justify their own speech while threatening the speech of others. He closes with a personal message to Revolution Muslims, singing "Go F#ck Yourself," complete with gospel choir.

By far the strongest response has been a viral Internet event called "Everybody Draw Muhammad Day." It was started by Seattle cartoonist Molly Norris, who created a fictional activist group called Citizens Against Citizens Against Humor who deemed May 20th the day for everybody to draw pictures of Muhammad and thereby water down the pool of potential targets. Although Molly herself pulled out of the event out of fear, "Everybody Draw Muhammad Day" has gone viral. Dan Savage featured the event on The Stranger. Michael Moynihan featured it at Reason.com. Suddenly there were Facebook groups and blog posts, and now the event is pressing on without its creator.

That is why I started with this verse from the Quran:

> And do not insult those whom they call upon instead of God, lest they insult God out of spite in their ignorance. We have made the deeds of each people fair seeming to themselves, and to their Lord is their return, and He will inform them of what they used to do. (Quran 6:108)

It's not a perfect fit, because we're talking about Muhammad, not Allah, and we're talking about a society's founding principles, not the gods they worship (although many arguably hold the US Constitution as a sacred document). But I think the verse fits because it demonstrates a really basic consequence at the root of this controversy. If Muslims are unjust toward non-Muslims, non-Muslims will respond with injustice out of spite. When Revolution Muslim escalated to threats of violence, the spiteful response escalated. Jon Wellington, who created the "Everybody Draw Muhammad Day" Facebook group, shut down the site. He said that it was originally intended to be a tribute to free expression, but it had turned into a forum of what he described as "deeply offensive pictures of the Prophet." We're not talking about bombs in turbans anymore. We're talking about satanic iconography and sexually explicit content. For many Americans these cartoons have become "fair seeming" because of the fear and intimidation created by Revolution Muslim and those who share their tactics. When Molly Norris pulled out of the event, she wrote on her website, "Personally, I can feel afraid of Muslims because I really have no idea if in their hearts they hate non-Muslims."

Clearly the *South Park* creators were trying to provoke a response, although I doubt they were hoping for a violent one. I think there is a serious discussion to be had about whether or not mockery of this kind is good for a society, but something I am absolutely certain of is that violence is not an appropriate tool to deter offensive speech. In fact, by inserting threats into the conversation, it is virtually impossible to criticize *South Park* without appearing to endorse violence. Similarly, it is almost impossible to criticize Revolution Muslim without appearing to endorse *South Park*. The moment the threat of violence enters the conversation, you can no longer have a civil discussion. But I'd like to try.

So what's the issue? There are two being conflated in this, and every other Muhammad cartoon fiasco. Is the problem depiction of Muhammad or criticism of Muhammad? They are being treated like they are the same thing, but they aren't. If Muslims are offended by Muhammad cartoons because Muhammad should not be depicted in Islam, then we should really be addressing the historical frieze of Prophet Muhammad on the North Wall of the US Supreme Court. There are also countless works of art throughout Islamic history that we need to answer for. It also raises the question why there was no controversy when *South Park* first debuted the Muhammad character in July 2001 as a member of "The Super Best Friends," a superhero team of religious figures who fight evil (except for Buddha, who doesn't believe in evil).

The fact is, none of the prophets should be depicted, according to Islamic doctrine. So, in theory, Revolution Muslim should have been sending threats the first time Jesus appeared on *South Park* years ago. In fact, Muslims should have stood alongside Christians offended by Andres Serrano's *Piss Christ* and Chris Ofili's depiction of the Virgin Mary covered in elephant dung. Did they? Islamically speaking, the taboo goes beyond prophets. No living things are supposed to be depicted. Islam is an aniconic religion. So in reality, if the issue is a religious objection to depiction, Muslims should be objecting to every cartoon everywhere. It seems like hypocrisy to play favorites with our outrage. So something else must be going on here.

Maybe it's about protecting the Prophet from criticism, as the *South Park* episode suggests. Muhammad is simultaneously the most beloved and the most reviled figure in history. Let's not pretend that that's insignificant. It is more socially acceptable to say slanderous and defamatory things about Muhammad and Islam than any other religious tradition. I'm not just talking about mockery and satire, I'm talking about real substantive hate speech. I live in a society where political figures like Tom Tancredo are cheered for suggesting we drop a nuclear bomb on Mecca, where Harvard professors like Martin Kramer advocate starving the Palestinian people to stop them from procreating; where bloggers like Robert Spencer, who practically regard my religion as a satanic cult, are regarded as experts on Islam. I think this is a social issue, not a legal one, but let's not pretend that Prophet Muhammad is not open to criticism.

So, what's going on here? If it's not depiction and it's not criticism, what is it? The genius of the *South Park* creators is that they were able to strike the root of the matter by isolating the variable. They never actually depicted the Prophet. It turns out that it was Santa Claus in the bear suit the whole time. And every image of Muhammad was censored. They also never actually criticized the Prophet. In the episode, he's something of a heroic figure who saves the town. He's treated respectfully. He's not insulted, or defamed. In fact, his only role in the show is to be in high demand. The most offensive thing in the episode, in my mind, was Buddha snorting cocaine. Yet Revolution

Muslim still leapt to the defense of Muhammad. Why?

To me it is now clear that it's not about Muhammad at all. Defending Muhammad is just a cloak of religious sanction these Muslims use to legitimize their behavior. Trey Parker and Matt Stone laid the trap, and Revolution Muslim jumped in. This episode was not a criticism of Muhammad, or a criticism of Islam, it was a criticism of the behavior of some Muslims. It was a punch in the ego of those Muslims who use intimidation and fear to impose their will on others. I am certain that this is what Kyle's final speech would have explained, and I hope the producers of *South Park* find some way of leaking it.

When things like this happen I am always reminded of an incident in the life of Ali ibn Abu Talib. It was during one of the battles with the Meccans. Ali had overpowered an enemy warrior, and had him on the ground ready to deliver a death blow. At that moment, the man spat in Ali's face. Ali responded by sheathing his sword, and releasing the man, which was utterly bewildering to him. When asked, Ali explained, "I only fight for the sake of God, and not for any private motive. When you spat in my face I became angry, and if I had killed you, it may have been from a desire for personal vengeance. So, rise and return to your people."

That is the kind of emotional discipline and self-knowledge that we need to develop in our community; and in my opinion, exploiting the religion to justify personal anger is a greater blasphemy than the cartoons themselves.

# Tea Party Muslims Shatter All Preconceptions

Muslims are terrorists who hate America's freedom... right? And the Tea Party are right-wing Christian extremists who hate Muslims... right? So, "Tea Party Muslim" must be a contradiction in terms, like "military intelligence" or "voluntary tax"... right? Well, that may be what the mainstream media would have you believe. After all, conflict sells. But one group is proving that Muslims and the Tea Party may have more in common than you think.

Will Coley describes himself as "your average camo-wearing, bow-hunting, East Tennessee redneck," except... he's also the director of Muslims 4 Liberty, a group of Muslims and non-Muslims of a liberty mindset fighting to change the perception of Islam in America, and offering tools to conservatives and libertarians who want the facts about Islam without all the sensationalized rhetoric we get in the mainstream media. Coley told me in an interview:

> We push libertarian ideas, constitutionalist ideas, and voluntaryist ideas in the Muslim community, and we do outreach to other Tea Party groups to say, "Look, we're here, we're not going anywhere, and we are fighting for liberty just like you. We should be fighting side by side, not against each other."

Coley has established his credibility in both camps. He is a longtime activist in the Tea Party movement, currently active in East Tennessee, and former co-host of *Tea Party Patriots Live* on WORL 660 Orlando, the first Tea Party radio program in America. He has also lectured at Valencia College and the University of Central Florida on Islamic history, interfaith relations, and Islamic law (Sharia). He is completing his training in Islamic studies and Sharia through a WebCT program in Qatar.

Muslims 4 Liberty has already achieved tremendous success in East Tennessee by launching educational classes at their local library, including a comparative study of Sharia and the US Constitution, which shows that they follow almost exactly the same guidelines, not only in form but in function. So far, twelve of the fourteen Tea Party groups in East Tennessee actually voted that the anti-Muslim hysteria should not be part of their message after Muslims 4 Liberty reached out to them. But Coley says the media isn't acknowledging their success. As he put it:

> The liberal media doesn't want to talk to us because we're Tea Party. The left doesn't want to admit that Muslim communities can work together with libertarians,

conservatives, and Republicans. The right-wing media isn't interested because we are Muslims and we believe in the principles of liberty as part of our faith. So we are the antithesis of this bogeyman they say we are. Basically our very existence challenges the narrative that both sides are using to create division in our society and maintain control.

Coley blames what he calls "The Jerry Springer Effect." The media are not genuinely interested in the truth—they are interested in selling advertising, so they will always focus the camera on the most provocative spectacle. When Ron Paul, regarded by many as the grandfather of the Tea Party, devotes his entire Congressional career to correctly predicting the economic and foreign policy quagmire we are in now, he is consistently ignored or ridiculed by the media. But when Jared Loughner kills a federal judge, and has even a tenuous connection to the Tea Party, that's the headline. Similarly, when extremist Anjem Choudary came to Washington DC to organize "Sharia Law in the USA" rallies, he got four days of royal treatment from the media, even though all three of his events were canceled when no one showed up except counter-protesters. But when 100 American imams organized an anti-terrorism rally the following weekend, which was attended by over a thousand Muslims, they got the Ron Paul treatment. Nobody covered it—not even the local media.

So, the Tea Party is dealing with the same problem as the Muslim community. They're struggling to wrestle their own narrative away from the media's agenda. But Coley is not taking rejection lying down. He says:

> You have to keep trying. That's the trick. You make one call and you find friends. You make another call and you find enemies. But you gotta keep making that next call.

Coley insists that libertarianism is spelled out in Sharia over and over again, from a constitutionally limited federal government and self-governed independent states, to the principles of free market economics and the protection of individual liberty. He calls what Anjem Choudary and others advocate "Saudi law," because there are no Sharia-compliant countries on Earth today, just places that drape a cloak of Sharia over their own corrupt un-Islamic systems.

He says Muslims support the ideas of the US Constitution because most of them came from English Common Law, which historically borrowed these ideas from the Saracens, the Muslims in Palestine. Legal concepts like the presumption of innocence, the inadmissibility of circumstantial evidence, and trial by jury have their origins in Sharia law. Even the Supreme Court has tremendous commonality with a court called the Qadi Mazalim in the Islamic system which has the power to nullify law and protect the people from the overreach of government.

Muslims support the free market because Muhammad himself was a merchant and practiced free market economics in his daily life. Muhammad taught that prices were set by God through the market, an uncanny parallel to Adam Smith's invisible hand. In addition, many Muslims advocate what they call "Sunnah money," which is identical to the gold standard advocated by libertarians.

In 2000, Muslims overwhelmingly voted for George W. Bush, in part because as a community they traditionally voted for conservatives, but also because Bush originally promised a "humble foreign policy with no nation building." Well... that didn't exactly work out. So in 2008, Muslims backed Barack Obama, who promised to close Guantanamo (still open) and to end the wars in Iraq and Afghanistan (still going). That didn't work out either. In fact, Obama killed more civilians in Muslim-majority countries in eighteen months than Bush had in seven years.

Coley reports that Muslims are defecting from Republicans *and* Democrats in droves because they have seen that both parties are willing to throw them under the bus the moment it's determined to be expedient. A portion of Muslims have become politically apathetic because they feel unrepresented, unwelcome, and as if they are not part of society. But many are joining libertarian, agorist, and voluntaryist groups. In fact, you may not even know when you're talking to a libertarian Muslim, because the libertarian philosophy is not about collectivism. Race and religious preference don't really matter in libertarian circles where you are judged by your principles and the content of your character.

Muslims 4 Liberty has people on staff with knowledge of Islam and Sharia who are currently focused on confronting the most vociferous anti-Muslim voices in America, like Pam Geller, Zuhdi Jasser, Robert Spencer, and others, and demanding that they prove what they claim. Coley says:

> We want an opportunity to expose these people for the fraud that they are, and show that they are spreading anti-Muslim hysteria for profit in our society.

So far, most of these so called "Sharia experts" have rejected Coley's invitations, which he believes is because they know that if they debate anyone with credentials it will expose them as charlatans.

# Texas Contractor Pimped Little Boys to Afghan Cops

WikiLeaks achieved international attention with its release of thousands of classified diplomatic cables leaked by Private First Class Bradley Manning. Many on the left and right, even in the State Department, are clamoring to have WikiLeaks declared a terrorist organization, with little regard to the actual definition of terrorism. They claim that the released information endangers the lives of some of the people named in the cables. Of course, the real reason, as we'll see, is that cockroaches can't stand the light. To the extent that revealing secret corruption endangers the lives of the corrupt, the onus of responsibility falls on the secret keeper, not the whistleblower. WikiLeaks is a "threat" because it challenges the secrecy on which authoritarian hegemony depends.

Here's an example:

Cable 09KABUL1651 from Kabul describes a meeting between US Assistant Ambassador Joseph Mussomeli and Afghan Minister Hanif Atmar on June 23, 2009. During the meeting, Atmar expresses concern that publicity over what he calls the "Kunduz DynCorp Problem" could "endanger lives." Sound familiar? He asks Mussomeli to "quash any news articles on the incident or circulation of a video connected with it."

So what is the Kunduz DynCorp Problem? What super-secret must be kept to protect lives?

DynCorp is the US corporation contracted by the US government to train the Afghan police force. Reportedly 95% of its $2 billion annual revenue comes from taxpayers. Well, some of that money was flowing into a child prostitution ring. On April 11, 2009, DynCorp apparently threw a party at the Kunduz Regional Training Center where prepubescent boys were dressed in women's clothing and made to dance seductively as they were auctioned as sex slaves.

It's called *bacha bazi* (literally "playing with children" in Persian), a pre-Islamic Afghan tradition that was banned by the Taliban.

Some "remedial disciplinary actions" were taken against DynCorp leaders in Afghanistan, and two Afghan National Police were charged with "purchasing a service from a child." The Afghan government proposed that a military officer be stationed to oversee DynCorp's facility... but that would violate the current DynCorp contract. Who thought giving sociopaths near-limitless revenue in a lawless region with no accountability was a good idea?

Of course the primary concern was a widely anticipated

newspaper article on the scandal. When the article appeared in *The Washington Post*, it said that DynCorp workers had "hired a teenage boy to perform a tribal dance at a company farewell party."

If anything, this is precisely why organizations like WikiLeaks are necessary. If an Afghan minister can leverage influence with a US diplomat to persuade a mainstream news outlet to report child sex slavery as "a tribal dance," how can the American people trust anything that's being reported to them?

The fact is, this is not DynCorp's first child-sex scandal.

In 1999 Kathryn Bolkovac was fired from DynCorp after blowing the whistle on a sex-slave ring on a US Army base in Bosnia. DynCorp employees were accused of raping and peddling girls from Ukraine, Moldova, and Romania, and forging documents to facilitate sex trafficking into Bosnia. In that case, DynCorp's Bosnia site supervisor filmed himself raping two girls.

In a move reminiscent of Catholic child-sex scandals, the offending employees were transferred to other bases, but no legal action was taken. Kathryn's book on the scandal, *The Whistleblower*, is available now, as is a movie of the same title.

In 2002, Ben Johnston, a DynCorp helicopter mechanic also in Bosnia, reported that other mechanics were boasting about sex slaves they had purchased from a local brothel. One DynCorp employee reportedly bragged, "My girl's not a day over twelve." Like Kathryn, Ben was fired, and no legal action was taken against the rapists.

In 2004, in Colombia, DynCorp employees distributed a video in which they raped and molested underage girls from the town of Melgar. The video was even distributed and sold to the general public, and one of the girls committed suicide after its release. No criminal investigation occurred.

DynCorp insists that it can't be held responsible, saying, "No company can guarantee that their employees will behave perfectly at all times." But it can be held responsible for what its lobbyists do. As reported in the *Chicago Tribune*, in 2006, DynCorp and Halliburton lobbyists worked together with the Pentagon to block legislation specifically banning sex trafficking by US contractors. The pentagon has yet to ban the practice.

There is an obvious conflict of interest when military contractors can lobby to stall legislation regulating their own behavior, but worse, it sure looks like these multi-billion-dollar military contractors actually condone child sex slavery, and spend tax dollars on it.

Oh, but Julian Assange is the terrorist for exposing it, not DynCorp for defending it.

# Bradley Manning Suffers "Unlawful Pretrial Punishment"

I've been saying for a while that the rights violations that American society allows to be perpetrated against American Muslims would one day be turned against the general population. It's just the nature of the State. Any power it is given is leveraged to secure more power. So, when you see them relaxing prohibitions on cruel and unusual punishments, eroding access to due process for Muslims, know that they are setting a precedent that will eventually extend to everyone. And now it has.

To some a hero, and others a traitor, Private First Class Bradley Manning has been held in a Marine brig in Quantico, Virginia, since May 2010 awaiting trial.

Bradley Manning has not been convicted of any crime.

In Quantico, Manning has been held as a "maximum custody detainee" under "Prevention of Injury watch," even though his captors admit that he has been a model detainee, without any disciplinary problems or episodes of disorder. He has demonstrated no threat to himself or others. This means that Manning spends 23 hours a day in intensive solitary confinement. He sits completely alone in a 6' x 12' cell, where he takes all his meals and sleeps on a bare mattress with no pillow or sheets. At night, he is stripped down to his underwear by guards who take his clothes until morning.

For one hour a day he is given exercise time, which means he is brought into a slightly larger room where he is only allowed to walk in figure-eights. Outside his cell he is placed in shackles. If he attempts to do push-ups or sit-ups in his cell, guards come in and physically prevent him from exercising, although he is permitted to stretch and is reportedly being allowed to practice yoga.

Bradley Manning has not been convicted of any crime.

Manning is completely deprived of human contact. Guards do not engage him in conversation, and he cannot interact with other inmates. He is not permitted any personal items except one book or magazine that has been reviewed by a literary board. He is reportedly reading *Decision Points* by George W. Bush, and occasionally the magazine *Scientific American*. For one hour a day, a television is wheeled in front of his cell and he's allowed to watch local news. He is permitted limited access to a pen and paper to exchange letters with family, but the only person he has been allowed to meet face to face is his attorney, David Coombs, who has expressed concern that extended isolation could have a detrimental effect on his client's psyche. He describes Manning's inhumane conditions as "unlawful pretrial punishment."

Bradley Manning has not been convicted of any crime.

Manning has spent over two and a half years in solitary confinement, which constitutes torture by the standards of many nations. The Geneva Conventions prohibit similar treatment of foreign prisoners. Prolonged solitary confinement violates the European Convention on Human Rights, and the Convention Against Torture, which bars EU states from extraditing people to any nation likely to utilize inhumane and degrading treatment.

Lieutenant Brian Villiard, a Quantico brig official, has said that Manning's conditions are likely to create long-term psychological injuries. As *The Journal of the American Academy of Psychiatry and the Law* puts it, "solitary confinement is recognized as difficult to withstand; indeed, psychological stressors such as isolation can be as clinically distressing as physical injury." The *Journal* states that "Psychological effects can include anxiety, depression, anger, cognition disturbances, perceptual distortions, obsessive thoughts, paranoia and psychosis."

A bipartisan National Commission on America's Prisons reported that psychiatric studies had found that prisoners held in prolonged isolation exhibited "a constellation of symptoms that includes overwhelming anxiety, confusion and hallucination, and sudden violent and self-destructive outbursts." The commission called for the elimination of prolonged solitary confinement. Extreme isolation of this kind has been described as "personality-erasing, soul-destroying, insanity-inducing conditions."

Bradley Manning has not been convicted of any crime.

*But Manning is a terrorist!* That's the constant mantra of the hawks who would burn the Constitution in order to persecute (I mean prosecute) him. According to chat logs prior to his arrest, Manning hoped the leak would lead to "worldwide discussion, debates, and reforms." He wrote:

> I want people to see the truth... because without information, you cannot make informed decisions as a public.

Even when it was suggested to him that he could get rich selling the cables to America's enemies, Manning insisted, "it belongs in the public domain—because another state would just take advantage of the information... try to get some edge. If it's out in the open... it should be a public good."

Far from being a terrorist, or a traitor against America, Bradley Manning demonstrates in his own statements that his intention is to better America, not harm it. Manning is a whistleblower in the truest sense, exposing corruption and secret malfeasance, seeking reform and correction through the political process.

Again, in the ever-expanding war on "terrorism," it is crucial to look at the precedent being set. Were it not for the precedents set in the treatment of Guantanamo Bay detainees, it is unlikely the American people would be so desensitized to the inhumane treatment of Bradley Manning. A century ago the Supreme Court consistently recognized extreme isolation as torture, comparing it, in the 1940 decision in *Chambers* v. *Florida*, to "the rack, the thumbscrew, and the wheel." But after a decade of national debate about whether water-boarding is torture, we've become calloused. If a whistleblower with the purest of motives can be imprisoned and tortured without trial or conviction, what precedents are being set for the future?

# A Brief History of the Fall of the Ottoman Caliphate

The Caliph was seated in Istanbul when the Ottoman Empire began to decline. The economy was penetrated by international bankers lending at high interest rates, and by 1896, debt had so infested the Ottoman economy that the Caliphate could not maintain the interest payments. Sultan Abdulhamid II was visited by Theodor Herzl, today regarded as the father of the Zionist movement. Using the same financial blackmail described in *Confessions of an Economic Hit Man* by John Perkins, Herzl offered to "negotiate" the loans of the Ottoman State in return for Palestine. Abdulhamid refused, but this death grip on the Ottoman economy allowed them to manipulate its policies, and eventually pressure them to enter into World War I against the better judgment of the Caliph.

During the war the British established two clients in Arabia. Hussein bin Ali, who was the appointed Shareef of Mecca, assisted the British against the Ottoman Empire in exchange for seven million pounds sterling. His rival, Abdul Aziz ibn Saud, who was allied with the Wahhabi movement in Riyadh, assisted the British for five thousand pounds sterling a month. The region of Arabia was not significant to the secular motivations of the war. The aim was to undermine the credibility of the Caliph by removing his control of the hajj, the annual religious pilgrimage to Mecca.

In 1917, when Edmund Allenby led the British army into Jerusalem, he said, "Today the Crusades have ended." Palestine remained a British territory until the secular state of Israel was established.

By 1919, the war was over and the Ottoman Empire was carved up by the Western powers. Iraq was created, Transjordan was created, Syria was created, Lebanon was created, and a new model of government emerged, as the Ottoman Caliphate was replaced by the Republic of Turkey. And in 1924, on orders from London, The Turkish National Assembly, led by Mustafa Ataturk, abolished the Caliphate.

It was not sufficient to abolish the Caliphate in Istanbul. It was necessary, before Israel could be established, to prevent the Muslims from reestablishing the Caliphate. In short, it was necessary to maintain control of Arabia, because no Caliph who could not control the hajj would be accepted by the Muslims. But Arabia could not be ruled directly by Western powers without a global uprising of Muslims. Instead it had to be ruled by a client state.

Four days after the Caliphate in Istanbul was abolished, Hussein bin Ali, the Shareef of Mecca, declared himself Caliph. Even though he helped the British during the war, now he'd crossed his British-Zionist handlers, whose objective was to emasculate the Muslim world so that the secular state of Israel could be established. In response, they put their support, both financial and military, behind Abdul Aziz ibn Saud, and the Wahhabi movement to attack Hussein and take control of Arabia. Although the Wahhabi movement claimed to represent the authentic teachings of Islam, Abdul Aziz ibn Saud did not claim the Caliphate. Instead they transformed the heartland of Islam into the modern state of Saudi Arabia, a European-style monarchy, which claimed divine sovereignty for itself. The Saudi-Wahhabi regime maintained the paraphernalia of an Islamic state, but was essentially a client of Western powers. Now no one can reestablish the Caliphate without gaining control of Mecca, and no one can control Mecca so long as the Saudis are supported militarily by Western powers. Further, the Saudis can't claim the Caliphate for themselves, because they are clients, and they know if they cross their American handlers, they will be destroyed.

Today we live in an age when an Islamic political order is impossible to restore until Arabia is liberated. But this cannot be done, as most Islamic movements attempt, by forming Islamic parties and working within the political system. The system itself is illegitimate because in order to achieve any success in the political process, you must bow to the constitution of that system, which declares the State sovereign.

# Chapter Eight: Arab Spring

## Spontaneous Order

"We will either live together, or we will die together."
—Mohamed El-Sawy, an Egyptian artist

On New Year's Day 2011, terrorists bombed a Coptic church in Egypt, killing twenty-one Christians. Those responsible were never identified, but it was assumed they were Muslim extremists intent on sowing religious strife. But by Coptic Christmas Eve a week later, thousands of Muslims acted as human shields to protect Christians as they attended Mass in churches around the country.

The following February, Coptic Christians returned the favor, joining hands to protect Muslims from police and pro-Mubarak thugs as protesters offered their Friday prayers in Tahrir Square. Then, Muslims did the same for Christians holding a memorial Mass in Tahrir Square to remember those who had been killed in the uprising.

Some called it the Egyptian Intifada. Everyone had their eye on Egypt as protests against the Mubarak regime swept the country.

More than anything, the lesson of the uprising was the efficacy of spontaneous order, the natural emergence of order out of chaos without central planning. As police in plainclothes picked fights and looted stores, civilians self-organized into neighborhood watch programs to protect each other. Several looters were even apprehended by civilians and discovered with government-issued weapons and badges.

There was this great lie in the reporting that the conflict was between "anti-government" and "pro-Mubarak" demonstrations. Police fire tear gas canisters (made in the US) and rubber bullets. Protesters throw rocks. The labels make it sound like we're talking about some kind of ideological difference, or partisan politics, but that's not it at all. The protests were about police brutality, political corruption, and economic exploitation. The "pro-Mubarak" crowd was not a rival populist movement. They were the brutal, the corrupt, and the exploiting class. They were Egypt's political parasites, who had reaped the benefits of the regime and wanted to keep the gravy train going.

As Mubarak obstinately refused to step down, he bleated on about maintaining stability and order. He reminds me of Chancellor Sutler in *V for Vendetta*, who said:

"What we need right now is a clear message to the people of this country. This message must be read in every newspaper, heard on every radio, seen on every television. This message must resound throughout the entire Interlink! I want this country to realize that we stand on the edge of oblivion. I want every man, woman, and child to understand how close we are to chaos. I want everyone to remember why they need us!"

See, the parasite class knows better than anyone just how little we need them. That's why, when they see the emergence of spontaneous order, they panic, and send out agents provocateurs to generate the chaos and instability that keeps them in control. It is only the self-determination of people that produces any true lasting peace.

# Moving Forward

When Mubarak announced he would not run for reelection, many of us who follow politics in the Middle East laughed at the implication that he had been legitimately elected in the first place. But Egyptians only escalated their peaceful protests until Cairo was packed like Mecca. Al Jazeera called it "The Woodstock of Egypt." When Mubarak officially stepped down, jubilation swept through the country over what may be the most non-violent revolution in history. Even here in the Bay Area at the Mosque I attend, they gave Takbirs for Egypt at Jummah prayer, served cake in celebration, and offered prayers for those who died to be accepted as martyrs.

But Egypt is not free yet.

Before stepping down, Mubarak appointed Omar Suleiman as vice president, and he is now waiting in the wings to seize the reins of power. He has long been the CIA's main man in Cairo, and to the Egyptians he is known as "The Minster of Torture." As the head of Egypt's national intelligence agency, Suleiman has overseen, and even directly participated in, the torture of detainees held without trial, often at the instruction of the US. But the greatest victory has already been won. The Egyptians have overcome their fear. They have stood up to tyranny and demanded liberty, and that is a genie not easily returned to the bottle.

Egypt and the US are going to have to redefine their relationship in light of recent events.

America's foreign policy template for Middle Eastern countries has been that the interests of Israel, and the flow of oil take precedence over all other concerns. There is a lip service paid to democracy, but whenever the people of these countries elect leaders who advocate policies that conflict with US interests, a coup is orchestrated, a dictator is installed, and mountains of American blood and treasure are expended securing these brutal regimes.

Historically this was done in the name of stability, but the long-term result has always been chaos, ending up in a situation where the governments of these countries support American interests, but every grass-roots movement, whether religious or secular, is boiling over with vitriol toward the US.

The problem with this policy is that tyranny inevitably falls to revolution—and when it does, the people remember who showered the dictator with gold and arms. The American government installed the Shah in Iran and got the Ayatollah. The tear gas canisters fired at protesters in Tahrir Square—"Tahrir," not so incidentally, means "Liberation"—were labeled "MADE IN AMERICA." The people of these nations don't hate America for our freedom. They hate America for empowering their tyranny.

So, how do we avoid this in the future? It's easy, really. Instead of trying to resolve the anti-American sentiment with military force and espionage, attempts should be made to address the root cause. Ironically, military force and espionage is the root cause. So, instead of conferring with Netanyahu in a smoky back room about who the next leader of Egypt should be, the US should categorically support self-determination for the Egyptian people, and agree to keep a diplomatic distance from whatever social order follows.

There's a lot of fear-mongering in American media that if Egyptians are allowed to determine their own destiny, they will choose an anti-American leader. Frankly, that's not relevant, and here's why: The anti-American sentiment is the symptom, not the cause. Even if the Egyptians chose an anti-American leader, that would also only be a symptom of American intervention. The cause, the reason that Egyptians have supported anti-American groups in the past, is that they were the only serious opposition to the Mubarak regime, which had the full support and backing of the US. If you remove that cause, the symptoms will eventually disappear. It may not happen instantly, but for long-term stability, it is the only peaceful solution.

# The Domino Effect

Paranoid talking heads were wringing their hands with worry that Egypt would become the next Iran. Now it seems that Iran is poised to become the next Egypt. Populist and pro-democracy protests have erupted all over the Middle East inspired by the revolutionary zeal in Tunisia and Egypt.

In February hundreds of thousands of protesters flooded into Tehran, the capital of Iran, chanting "Death to the dictator." They were met by riot police, and many were injured. The Iranian government blamed the violence on "agitators and seditionists."

Thousands of Algerians swarmed the center of Algiers, where they confronted a massive deployment of riot police.

In Sanaa, the capital city of Yemen, riot police clashed with thousands of pro-democracy protesters demanding the resignation of President Ali Abdullah Saleh. This was the fourth consecutive day of anti-government rallies in Yemen's Tahrir Square, which shares the name with Cairo's gathering place.

In Bahrain, thousands of protesters observed a "Day of Rage" in the capital of Manama and were assaulted with tear gas and rubber bullets by riot police.

After a number of minor protests were quashed by the Saudi government, a Mufti named Sheikh Yusof al-Ahmad warned that Saudi Arabia would face a revolution similar to those in Egypt and Tunisia if the government didn't address the people's demands.

As far as I can tell, all of these are pro-democracy movements, or at the very least self-determination movements. Egyptian opposition leader George Ishak said, "We have proved Mubarak and his regime wrong, and we will now show the world how we will build a real democracy." After his Friday sermon, Sheikh Muhammad al-Azhari said, "This was the first time in my life I was able to speak freely from the pulpit without fear of reprisal." Whatever comes of these uprisings, whatever system emerges, there is no question that this represents a dramatic increase in liberty in these countries.

It seems that peaceful protesters armed with WikiLeaks and Facebook can do for themselves in a month what the US military failed to do for Iraq and Afghanistan in ten years.

# Democratization

With all the uprisings in Egypt, Iran, and elsewhere, it seems clear we are witnessing the slow democratization of the Middle East. The framers of the American system drew upon all of history in their deliberation. Likewise, there is no reason that democracy in the Middle East must emulate the democracies of the West when they could learn from America's history and avoid problems so deeply entrenched they will never be solved here. To paraphrase Thomas Paine, they have it in their power to begin the world over again.

### Old Technology:
The promise of democracy is that government represents the Will of the people. If anything has been proven by recent history it is that Internet access is superior to ballot access in organizing and implementing collective Will. The election process is old technology, especially structures like the Electoral College that are nothing but an artifact of a horse-and-buggy world. Modern technology could make expressing public Will virtually instantaneous. Tracking public opinion could happen constantly, rising and falling like trending topics on Twitter. Political platforms could be as accessible as Facebook profiles. Skype could open every smoky back room deal to public scrutiny. Elections could look more like *The Apprentice*, with a dozen candidates testing their leadership prowess in elimination-style competition. And I'm sure WikiLeaks would have a field day with the behind-the-scenes footage. Democracy in the Middle East could easily be a Democracy 2.0.

Putting that aside, I would suggest that democracy is not the panacea it is made out to be. In fact, it's fraught with problems. Keep in mind Soviet socialism, Italian fascism, and German Nazism all grew out of democracies. As the saying goes, democracy is two wolves and a sheep deciding on dinner—and liberty is an armed sheep contesting the vote.

### The Tragedy of the Commons:
It's a well-known phenomenon that when something is owned in common, and no individual bears the burden of responsibility, it is mismanaged. In these situations, each individual is incentivized to prioritize short-term gains over long-term sustainability. In a democracy, leaders are temporary and bear virtually no personal responsibility for their decisions. As a result, politicians tend to exploit their position in the short term, pushing the long-term consequences off on future generations. Far from preventing this phenomenon, the

people are complacent beneficiaries of it. Voters demand ever-increasing government handouts, while simultaneously insisting on lower taxes. To accommodate this, the national debt must be increased. In essence, the only way to get elected is to bribe the current electorate by mortgaging the future wealth of the unborn. The end result is always complete collapse.

### The Tyranny of the Majority:
Democracy is "majority rules," which is contradictory to individual freedom because the Will of the majority is enforced upon the individual without consent. Here's what I mean: In a survey of the most popular ice cream flavors, vanilla was the favorite, scoring 29%. Chocolate was second with 8.9%. Butter pecan was third with 5.3%. The remaining 56.8% (a majority of the population) preferred a wide variety of other flavors. In a free system, vanilla may earn the largest market share, but the other flavors are still widely available. In a democratic system, vanilla would be "The People's Flavor" and it would become criminal to consume other flavors. This is the reality that is seldom presented to voters. When you vote, you aren't just expressing your preferences, you are asking the government to force your preferences on your neighbor. You are electing a monopoly.

### The Dogs of War:
Democracies wage war in a way radically different from other forms of government. War is essentially fought over resources and territory. In monarchies and dictatorships, organized armies confront one another, and to the victor go the spoils. This creates an incentive to preserve civilian life and infrastructure, because ultimately capturing the tax base is the goal. In democracies, politicians have dual loyalties to the military–industrial complex, which wants war, and to the people, who don't. So, to satisfy both, war must be fought for ideological reasons against intangible concepts. The people don't want war for treasure, but they can be rallied to fight "Communism" and "Islamofascism." The result is total war. There is no longer a territory to conquer, or an army to vanquish. Now the enemy is an idea that can be harbored by anyone. So, "collateral damage" becomes a necessary part of war. A democracy must even view its own citizens with suspicion.

Freedom is self-determination. Democracy provides this illusion at a national level, but individual freedom always disappears into an avalanche of legislation. The people's wealth is eroded by ever-increasing taxes, monetary inflation, and insurmountable national debt. And the system itself inevitably collapses under its own weight.

So, I have an idea: As these Middle Eastern tyrants step down, or are overthrown, how about if no one steps up? Imagine if, instead of electing another violent monopoly, the Egyptians allowed the spontaneous order currently emerging to freely take shape. People are already voluntarily cooperating to resolve their problems and provide necessary services, not only in the absence of government, but in spite of the government.

While police were releasing violent criminals from prison following the confusion of the protests, the youth of Egypt took up pipes and broom handles to protect their neighborhoods from looters. Residents said it was the safest they had ever felt. In less than two weeks, free people spontaneously found ways to protect themselves without coercive taxation, or an elected monopoly, or a police force.

During the protest there were food shortages that resulted in supermarket runs. You might expect that situation to result in fistfights, but people organized community potlucks. Medical professionals, many of whom were unemployed or working as taxi drivers under the regime, volunteered their services to help those injured by riot police. After the protests, hundreds of volunteers came together to sweep, scrub, and paint the square.

Perhaps the most unsung heroes of the Egyptian Revolution are the dozens of plumbers who helped divert water from the mosque to build working bathrooms, and kept the public toilets of Tahrir Square functioning properly. All of this was done without permits, without tax dollars, without politicians, and without voting.

If there is any lesson to learn from this, it is just how effective the people are at problem-solving when they are simply free to do so. Saying that removing Mubarak creates a power vacuum is like saying that removing a cow from the freeway creates a cow vacuum. The people don't need the government to structure society for them. They just need for it to stay out of the way. The flow of traffic will correct itself.

# Chapter Nine: Occupy

## Solidarity: Can the Tea Party and Occupy Wall Street Find Common Cause?

Many libertarians will point out that the definition of "liberal" has changed over time. What used to be a philosophy of small government and economic freedom is now the hallmark of a busybody nanny state and central economic planning. To clarify the distinction, many call themselves "classical liberals." What's less often discussed is the history of "solidarity." Today "solidarity" is used to mean unity among international socialists and communist organizations. At rallies they espouse messages of peace, diversity, and freedom—which I stand behind—but their literature usually preaches a dictatorship of the proletariat.

The history of "solidarity" is quite different however. In Poland the term "Solidarność" was used to describe a non-governmental trade union, or more accurately a black market resistance movement operating within the Soviet Bloc in the 1980s. Solidarity was a non-violent, anti-communist movement that was instrumental to the fall of the Soviet Union, and it could easily be described as a "classical liberal" movement. In 1986, free market economist Murray Rothbard visited Poland with warm reception from Solidarity, and the movement was flush with translations of Ludwig von Mises and Friedrich Hayek, which were contraband.

One lesson to be learned from this is the folly of Utopianism. Prior to Solidarity's inception, many anti-Soviet groups held the erroneous belief that a movement must hold a Utopian ideal to keep activists motivated. The result was infighting between groups who shared the same immediate goal, but different long-term goals. In short, Utopianism made them easy to divide and conquer. Solidarity proposed a different strategy whereby the emphasis was not on what activists favored, but instead on a broad agreement as to what they opposed. This was equally motivating, but without the divisiveness.

Fast-forward to today and the world is erupting in dazzling explosions of populist movements. Tunisia, Egypt, London, and now Wall Street. They all have different goals, but they all oppose the same thing, which is entrenched power structures. I view them as the natural emergent order resulting from the proliferation of the Internet. Cyberspace is rapidly re-creating meatspace in its own image. Old strategies must adapt or perish, and one of those strategies whose time has come is Utopianism.

There are arguably two populist movements in the US right now: Occupy Wall Street and the Tea Party. Most first-wave Tea Partiers readily acknowledge that their organization has already been hijacked. During the Bush Administration, the Tea Party had two goals: to end the wars in the Middle East and to abolish the Federal Reserve. Both of these could easily rally bipartisan populist support, but once Obama was elected, they flipped the script and it became about opposing Obamacare, or the Ground Zero Mosque, or illegal immigration, or whatever current cause local politicians found it advantageous to exploit. Similarly, Occupy Wall Street began like all populist movements, as an attempt to confront entrenched power structures. They specifically aimed "to separate money from politics" and to "take to task the people who perpetrated the economic meltdown." The End the Fed movement was well represented in their ranks.

It's clear, at least to me, that both of these movements contain both a Solidarity wing and a Utopian wing, in the classic Polish sense. If you look at the first demands published on the OccupyWallSt.org forum, they are ripe for hijacking by Utopians. They want, among other things, to raise the minimum wage to $20/hour, to institute a universal healthcare system by banning all private insurance, and forgiveness for all debt, both national and personal. But there's also an "Occupy the Federal Reserve" call on the same site, which both movements could embrace.

Imagine this: What would happen if the Tea Party crowd and the Occupy Wall Street crowd came to a general consensus that the system itself is broken, and that the people are no longer in control of this government? What if they agreed that the government was no longer a servant but a mercenary? Can they both agree that avoiding plutocracy takes precedence over all their pet issues? If so, do these movements have the discipline to reexamine their own platforms, and, when they disagree, to set those issues aside as Utopian for now, and instead form a broad solidarity on the issues where they agree?

I guarantee you that nothing is more terrifying to the entrenched power structure than a broad solidarity between the populist movements of the left and the right. And I guarantee you that it works long nights devising ways to hijack these movements and pit them against each other.

The slogan of Occupy Wall Street has become "We Are the 99%." Will they restrict themselves to those issues upon which 99% of us agree?

# The Day of the Barricades

At a Congressional hearing, Federal Reserve Chairman Ben Bernanke commented on the Occupy movement, saying, "They blame, with some justification, the problems in the financial sector for getting us into this mess, and they're dissatisfied with the policy response here in Washington. And at some level, I can't blame them." But *they* can certainly blame *him*! On the streets of San Francisco, Occupants are calling out Ben Bernanke by name, demanding that he be prosecuted and imprisoned for what they say amounts to treason and crimes against humanity.

I spent three days and two nights sleeping on the streets at the OccupySF camp when it was still set up. What began with six people sitting in front of the San Francisco Federal Reserve building exploded to 800 protesters completely blocking off Market Street after the first raid.

Before the raid, OccupySF consisted of approximately 200 Occupants in a tent city on the Federal Reserve building grounds. The encampment included a working kitchen with propane-powered stove, a communications center with power generator, and an infirmary. All provisions from food to medical supplies had been donated by supporters. Although originally promised that tents would be allowed, prior to the raid, orders came from the SFPD that they would need to be taken down. The Occupants complied with these orders.

At 2:00 AM on Thursday, October 6th, 2011, approximately eighty officers wearing riot gear raided the encampment anyway. Police formed a perimeter separating the Occupants from their supplies as the Department of Public Works seized nine truckloads of tents, communications equipment, medical supplies, food, and other donations.

About fifty Occupants responded with peaceful resistance, standing in front of the trucks and forming a human chain to impede the city from stealing their supplies. Police responded by cracking skulls.

Only one arrest was made, but at least three Occupants sustained injuries. including a 17-year-old girl who was punched and thrown to the ground simply for standing too close to the police line. One officer reportedly told another Occupant, "I can't wait to beat your face in."

The American Civil Liberties Union (ACLU) and the National Lawyers Guild (NLG) helped OccupySF explore their legal options. Many argued that the raid on the encampment, and the demands themselves, were not in accordance with law. After the raid, the police erected a metal barricade blocking off the Federal Reserve grounds, and stationed officers on guard around the clock. OccupySF pledged to hold the occupation on the wide sidewalk in front of the Federal Reserve, and issued the following statement the next morning:

> Last night the SFPD issued us an unsigned, undated notice that declared we had to pack up our tents without giving us a timeline or else we would risk arrest. They said that we could remain occupying if we pulled down our tents and complied with their other demands. We complied with their demands by taking down our tents and beginning to clear-out the rest of our infrastructure that was allegedly in violation of city and/or state laws. We made a call to action. Our numbers doubled within half an hour. Yet still, the police, wearing helmets and carrying batons, formed a perimeter around our goods and prevented us from saving anything while they supervised Public Works employees as they stole everything. The police stole food, water, shelter, and other necessities of life from the 99% at OccupySF.

After the ACLU and NLG involvement, police received orders from above to respect the peaceful Occupants. The camp was informed that they would not be permitted to build any tent structures or cook any food, but would be permitted to occupy the space.

# Locke vs. Marx

It didn't take more than a night at OccupySF to realize that the core group of Occupants consisted of deeply committed young socialists, communists, and social anarchists. In fact, the magazine that started this whole Occupy movement, *Adbusters*, is arguably an anarcho-communist rag. Now, I have a lot of love for that crowd, because to some degree, this is my background, and I understand that they are coming from a well-meaning place. Dyed hair, dreadlocks, facial piercings, and tattoos are all common. We used to call it "gutter punk." I'm not sure if that's a pejorative term now. I certainly don't mean it that way. They are homeless young adults who are voluntarily unemployed as an act of rebellion against capitalism.

This indicates that, potentially, the Occupation could go on for a long, long time. They are accustomed to life on the streets. During the day, the Occupation triples, and more mainstream political perspectives prevail; but at night, the crowd goes home and it's the anarchists who hold the ground, moderate the General Assemblies, and ultimately decide how to spend the donations. Why would they ever leave? This is the lifestyle they have chosen.

One night I stayed up until dawn talking with a young Marxist. We distilled all our political and economic disagreements down to one philosophical split that we couldn't resolve: I believe in private property and he doesn't.

I generally take something like the Lockean view. In John Locke's *Second Treatise*, he argues that the individual ownership of property derives from the mixing of labor with nature to produce goods. The Marxist argued that because goods were originally part of the commons, to claim individual ownership in anything was to steal from everyone else—echoing that famous social anarchist cry, "Property is theft." So, according to this viewpoint, all goods must always be owned in common. We discussed a number of thought experiments to see if we could parse out the disagreement.

### Scenario One:
Two men come upon an uninhabited valley and each develops separate plots into farmland. One man grows apples and the other grows oranges. Do the men own what they produce individually or in common? A Lockean would say each farmer owns the fruits of his own labor. He may trade his produce, or give it away, but the decision is his how to allocate his own produce. The Marxist says that both farmers own all the fruit. From my perspective, if someone else has an ownership claim on the fruits of my labor, that's akin to owning my

labor, which is akin to owning my body, which is akin to slavery. We could not reach an agreement in this scenario, so we changed the parameters.

### Scenario Two:

Two men come upon a valley where they discover a plot of farmland where someone has already grown a crop of tomatoes, but the farmer is not there. Do the two men own the tomatoes in common? In other words, is it appropriate for the two men to eat the tomatoes without asking? Initially the Marxist said no, that they should respect the farmer by finding him and asking permission. So I pointed out that that was respecting the farmer's property rights. It didn't make any sense to ask permission unless the farmer had more authority to grant permission to eat the tomatoes than the two men. Then the Marxist changed his answer and said yes, they have a right to eat the tomatoes without asking because the crop of tomatoes was more than the needs of one farmer. So I pointed out that they may be eating food that was intended for the farmer's children.

This flustered the Marxist, who then protested that hypothetical scenarios are irrelevant because there is no pure, justly acquired property in the real world. All land has been stolen and all goods are made with exploited labor. So we stopped using hypothetical scenarios.

### Scenario Three:

I carry a knife in my pocket. It doesn't fit the definition of justly acquired property for the Marxist. It was probably assembled by child labor in China or something. Yet I have a subjective sense that I own it, because the concept of ownership only requires that I have a stronger claim on the knife than the Marxist does. If I hand the knife over to the Marxist, that doesn't resolve whatever injustice occurred in its manufacturing. So I asked him if he felt that he had as strong a claim on the knife as I did. In other words, is it appropriate for him to take it from me, or to use it without my permission?

At first he tried to tell me that I only felt I owned the knife because we were in a capitalist system, and in a communist system there would be such an abundance of knives I would feel no need to assert any ownership of it. But that's not true. Even if there were a communist knife shop someplace giving away free knives, that's still farther away than my own pocket, and traveling to the free knife shop still constitutes mixing the knife with my labor. I would still feel some claim on the knife that I retrieved because I wouldn't want to walk back to the shop over and over. But, we had agreed, no more hypotheticals.

The Marxist reluctantly conceded that I owned my knife, and he had no right to take it from me.

Ironically, the gutter punks who preach against the concept of ownership all behave as if they believe in ownership in the real world. They get upset when their possessions go missing. They ask permission when they want to use other people's things, and they return items when they are finished.

It's always important to remind people that on the road to a classless, stateless society, Marx was calling for a "dictatorship of the proletariat" where all private property was first subsumed by the State before it was returned to the commons.

# General Assemblies and Consensus-Building

By far the most fascinating and innovative aspect of the Occupy movement has been the social structure they've developed. Obviously I can only speak about what I have directly witnessed at OccupySF, but I've been told these strategies are similar throughout the movement, including a strong consensus against the establishment of any leader or hierarchy.

Every day there is a General Assembly in which proposals and announcements can be made by all participants. After the Day of the Barricades, the General Assembly was so large that it had to be moved to the Ferry Building, where guest speakers from the ACLU and NLG offered legal assistance such as Know Your Rights workshops, direct action training, tactical discussions, legal observer training, and copwatch training. These meetings are not being organized by a majority-rules democratic process—instead they've evolved to incorporate a number of tools for crowd-sourcing decision-making by consensus.

General Assemblies are moderated by a volunteer, but all participants have the power of veto. They have also developed a language of hand signals that allow the crowd to express their support or disapproval of the speaker's message. Forming an "X" above your head signals disapproval, while wiggling your fingers above your head signals applause without the disruptive sound. If a decision ever must be made by an up-or-down vote, a thumbs-up or -down is sufficient—but the decision is not made by the majority. Instead, every individual has the power to *block*. If it's all thumbs-up, they call it a *consensus*. But if someone blocks, they are given the floor to express their objection until a consensus can be reached.

Obviously this process can be messy and time-consuming. For example, the culture in San Francisco is very anti-smoking, and there was a strong desire by some to ban smoking in the camp—but no consensus could be reached. After a few minor confrontations, this was resolved by polite requests and respectful distances. No hard fast rules were necessary. New customs were sufficient.

Many of the innovations have also been a response to police aggression.

The Occupants had been using a gas-powered electric generator to charge laptops and phones, and run the live feed equipment in the communications center. During the raid, police seized the generator, and then forbade the camp to use the replacement generator that had been donated, allegedly because of noise and health concerns over the exhaust. Occupants responded by constructing a bicycle-powered generator connected to a series of car batteries hooked up to a plug strip. They invited people to "donate their rage," channeling

their frustration into pedaling the bike, which in turn charged the batteries and provided the camp with electricity. In fact, it's only because of this innovation that I was able to blog from the camp.

Police said that Occupants couldn't use amplified sound, although megaphones were still in evidence during active protests and marches. But the rest of the time they used something they'd developed called "the People's Mic." Anyone in the camp may call out, "Mic Check!" and all Occupants within earshot echo back "Mic Check!" Once the speaker has the attention of the camp, he begins to make his announcement in small segments allowing the crowd to echo the statement in unison, in effect amplifying the sound without any amplification device.

Before the raid, the camp had appointed a "police liaison" to carry messages to and from the police department. After the raid, there was so much animosity toward the police, and so much backtalk to the police liaison that it was decided the position was too similar to a leader, and the Occupants demanded that the police address the group as everyone else does, by using the People's Mic.

So strong is the rejection of leadership and hierarchy, at least in this crowd, that there is a general rejection of codifying the message of the group into a list of demands. This is thought to be exclusionary and limiting of the diversity of the movement. In fact, one afternoon a couple arrived, rolled out a big piece of butcher paper, and began hand-writing a proposed list of demands that had gone viral from the Occupy Wall Street forum. There was immediate backlash from the Occupants, who insisted that this couple had no right to speak on behalf of the community, that there was no consensus on this list of demands in OccupySF, and that the original list was the work of one person on a forum, not even the consensus of Occupy Wall Street. In the end, the couple posted the list among all the other signs, but was not permitted to claim that it represented the consensus of the group, and many other Occupants posted amendments next to the list expressing their respectful disagreement.

Whatever this thing is developing into, it is unlike anything we've seen.

# Can the Occupy Movement Break the Grip of the Money Trust?

Many regard Dennis Kucinich as the Ron Paul of the left. The two men have shown tremendous respect and solidarity with each other over the years. In a public statement of support for the Occupy movement, Dennis Kucinich took aim at what is perhaps Ron Paul's signature issue, the Federal Reserve. Similarly, the Occupy movement is waking up to what was a central issue to the first wave of the Tea Party, the fiat monetary system.

It seems as though liberal critique of the Federal Reserve is not that fiat currency is inherently fraudulent, but that it's being exploited by private interests. They don't really want to abolish the Federal Reserve, but to nationalize it, which is problematic. Some Occupants are calling for a "Reserve Bank of America," which would be regulated by "the elected government of the 99%." They ignore the fact that the Federal Reserve Act of 1913 was passed by that very government. I'd like to offer all my new Occupant friends a brief primer on the Federal Reserve for those new to the party.

In the early 1900s, the American people were very concerned about something they called the "Money Trust," which was the concentration of financial power in the hands of Wall Street and big banks. Sound familiar? Numerous candidates were elected on the campaign promise to "break the grip of the Money Trust." One such candidate was Senator Nelson Aldrich, who was appointed chairman of the National Monetary Commission formed to address the people's concerns.

In 1910, Senator Aldrich convened a secret meeting between six of the most powerful financial elites in the world. Historians tell us that between them, these seven men controlled 25% of the wealth of the entire world. The seven had been competitors, at each other's throats, but Senator Aldrich brought them together and formed a banking cartel. Unlike other cartels, this one also went into partnership with the government, and the seven of them drafted the Federal Reserve Act.

Aldrich handed the cartel's bill over to their cronies in Congress, both Republicans and Democrats, and then these same financial elites immediately went to the media and publicly begged Congress not to pass the bill, crying that it would ruin the banking industry. Their phony protestations translated into overwhelming support for the legislation from the people, who despised the big banks. The people were told that the bill would finally "break the grip of the Money Trust"—but they didn't know the bill was *written* by the Money Trust.

The bill passed in 1913, creating the Federal Reserve, and transferring the monopoly power to issue money from the US Treasury to those very financial elites. This is not a conspiracy theory— this is undisputed historical fact: All this information was published in their own memoirs.

Since 1913, the Federal Reserve has gradually and systematically separated the monetary unit from its commodity backing. In 1972 it was completely severed, becoming a fiat currency, which is a paper (or digital) note that has no intrinsic value. This means that the Federal Reserve can increase the money supply at will, which is the cause of inflation. We experience rising prices not because the real cost of goods increase, but because the purchasing power of the dollar decreases. Since 1913 the dollar has lost 97% of its purchasing power.

It's important that my liberal friends understand that the government is complicit in this fraud, because it directly benefits from it. The banking cartel benefits because it allows them to charge interest at rates they set on money they create out of thin air. In other words, to profit without work. But the government benefits because the Federal Reserve offers them limitless credit to fund their unpopular projects without directly taxing the people. The result is inflation, which is an invisible tax that attacks the poor worst of all. So, for example, we experience the cost of war as a recession instead of a war tax, which obfuscates the root cause of poverty and causes people to blame the businesses that are forced to raise their prices instead of the monetary policy that is eroding our wages. The recession is a war tax taken through inflation.

One of the major problems with this system is that all money is created by the Federal Reserve and then lent to the government. But there is interest on that loan, which means there is never enough money in existence to actually pay the debt. This means that the collateral on that loan is you, your future earnings, and the future earnings of your children.

If you nationalize the Federal Reserve without abolishing fiat money, it resolves the government's interest payment problem, but not the inflation problem—which disproportionately hurts the poor because the wealthy don't store their wealth in dollars, but in commodities to protect themselves from inflation. That's what Wall Street is. That's why Wall Street is what it is. Fiat money leads to hyper-inflation regardless of who has their hand on the printing press. Nationalizing the Federal Reserve would only remove whatever checks still exist on the creation of money.

The Occupy movement wants to break the grip of the Money Trust, but doesn't understand that placing financial power in the hands of elected officials isn't any different. I don't know where this trust of government comes from. Remember, the Federal Reserve originally came about when the people asked their elected officials to break the grip of the Money Trust—and look what they gave us! Congress is unlikely to vote against their own limitless credit.

If you want to put the financial power in the hands of the people through their elected governments, why not put the financial power in the hands of the people directly? Why not repeal all legal tender laws that force people to conduct commerce in dollars, and allow everyone to use whatever medium of exchange they like?

# When Police Go *State*

Chris Rock once said, "That tiger didn't go crazy. That tiger went *tiger!*" Well, in Oakland, the police department went *State*. Over 500 officers and sheriffs' deputies from over twelve agencies assisted the Oakland Police Department in a pre-dawn raid of OccupyOakland, evicting Occupants from the newly named Oscar Grant Plaza in front of Oakland City Hall. Riot police clad in gas masks used rubber bullets, beanbag rounds, flash grenades, tear gas canisters, and an LRAD sonic cannon against non-violent protesters. There were mass arrests, and although the police reported that there were no injuries, live Twitter accounts disagree. City officials advised downtown businesses to remain closed the rest of the day.

The Occupants were not unprepared for this eventuality and were ready with an "emergency re-convergence plan," beginning with an emergency assembly later that day at the Oakland Public Library.

One of the first eyewitness accounts came from Kevin Army, a journalist I met at the OccupyOakland encampment. He reported that when the police lined up before the raid, he attempted to capture video when officer #570 shouted and rammed into him, pushing him to the ground. He was told by a commanding officer to stand in a designated area with the mainstream media. After the police had herded all the media together, Kevin reports, they were shot with tear gas, disbursed, and not allowed to return to cover the raid. He believed this was intentional.

Before the raid, OccupyOakland had been dubbed a "demilitarized zone." While OccupySF had faced raids and police brutality from its inception, the City of Oakland had been exceptionally welcoming of the encampment. They were permitted to set up over 150 tents. The encampment had portable toilets and garbage service. They had both first-aid and childcare tents. They even hosted live music and screened films with a projector on a theater-sized screen. Although there were isolated reports of fights, drug use, and sexual harassment—such is Oakland—the encampment's General Assemblies were already organizing autonomous solutions to these problems. A leaderless patrol of ten to twenty Occupants originally formed to run twenty-four-hour "cop watch" for the encampment were working to defuse fights, discourage hard drug use, and protect women and queer Occupants from sexual harassment. OccupyOakland had become more than an organized protest—it was an experiment in self-governance, addressing many of the systemic problems the City of Oakland ignores. For nearly two weeks, not a single person went hungry in Oakland, and many of the city's homeless population reported a sense of safety in the encampment not felt anywhere else in the city.

Friday afternoon, the city posted an eviction notice saying that those who stayed would be subject to arrest because "neither the demonstrators nor the City could maintain safe or sanitary conditions." Karen Boyd, a spokesbureaucrat for the mayor, told the *Oakland Tribune* that "the protesters had shown themselves incapable of self-governance." But that's patently false. All the city's complaints were already being spontaneously handled by the Occupants. This raid, in my opinion, was conducted precisely because the protesters were showing that they *were* capable of self-governance, and both police and city officials were terrified of showing the average citizen just how unnecessary governmental institutions really are. Occupants had no intention of leaving, deciding at the next General Assembly to defend the encampment. Several hundred Occupants worked to block off the entrances to the plaza using Dumpsters, wooden pallets, and even police-style metal barricades in the hours before the raid.

At 3:00 AM on Tuesday, October 25th, 2011, police cars patrolled the streets around the plaza, and helicopters lit up the area from above. The raid began at 4:40 AM, when 170 remaining Occupants locked arms as hundreds of police officers from multiple Bay Area cities surrounded them and moved in. The invaders fired tear gas and beanbag rounds at the non-violent Occupants and ultimately arrested seventy-five for "misdemeanor illegal lodging." Police ripped apart the tents and threw them in the street. According to authorities, the plaza was "contained" by 5:30 AM.

Neither defeated nor discouraged, the Occupants knew this aggression from the city would only translate into more public support.

# Of Rebels and Tear Gas

After the pre-dawn raid, the displaced Occupants performed an impromptu march through downtown Oakland and eventually returned to the destroyed campsite, where they faced off with officers. What had begun with a few hundred Occupants quickly grew into thousands attempting to reclaim the plaza.

During the march a young woman was pulled into the police line and slammed onto the ground by two huge officers. Protesters covered these officers with water balloons filled with paint, mimicking the paintballs police shoot at protesters to mark people of interest. Low-flying helicopters followed the crowd through Oakland. Police blocked off main thoroughfares, diverting the march into side streets.

The march returned briefly to Snow Park, which was a backup location for the Occupation, but ultimately the Occupants decided to make their stand at the plaza, which was blocked by multiple layers of metal barricades, and line after line of riot police. Every side entrance was also barricaded and guarded by riot police standing shoulder to shoulder in two or more rows. That night, Oscar Grant Plaza was the best-protected empty field I've ever seen.

Occupants immediately rushed the line and grabbed hold of the first row of barricades, dragging them into the street (and, incidentally, knocking me over). Police began repeating over the loudspeaker, "This is the Oakland Police Department. This has been declared an illegal assembly. Immediately leave now! If you do not, you are subject to removal by whatever force necessary, which may result in serious injury." The crowd only laughed, and many began to lie down in the intersection in front of the plaza.

A lone Navy veteran stood toe-to-toe with the police line, waving the flag of Veterans for Peace.

Police began firing tear gas, flash bombs, and percussion grenades into the crowd. The protest disbursed, if only temporarily. Tear gas is nasty! It's like rubbing a fistful of wasabi in your eyes. The Occupants in wheelchairs got it much worse than me, but the last to leave was that lone Navy veteran, who stood in the front line and then walked through the tear gas calmly, seemingly unaffected. He must have had special training. It looked like a scene out of an action film.

Scott Olsen, a former Marine and member of Veterans for Peace, had come home safe from Iraq, but earned his Purple Heart in Oakland. He was struck in the face by a canister fired at him by police. Those who tried to help him were shot with rubber bullets and flash-bang grenades. Scott was unconscious and hospitalized in critical condition, suffering from brain swelling.

Oakland looked identical to photos of the Arab Spring that night.

The protest was scattered at that point. Divided groups walking back and forth between the plaza and Snow Park. Scattered reports of more tear gas and flash-bang grenades throughout the night. Small patrols of riot police stationed on almost every side street. Formations of riot cops clearing streets block by block.

Ultimately everyone ended up back at the plaza, and at some point someone threw a bottle at the cops. The crowd immediately began chanting "Don't throw shit!" The person was eventually identified and scolded by other Occupants.

I have to say something about this. The young revolution enthusiasts out there say that force should be met with force. I have no moral objection to this, although I think it tactically stupid, but when you have a crowd that has an overwhelming consensus that they are non-violent and non-retaliatory, and that's a central part of their message and strategy, if you provoke the beast and then disappear into the crowd, you are a coward. You endanger the lives and bodily integrity of others when you should be taking responsibility for your own risky behavior. The police response to such actions is completely predictable, and when you take such an action in a crowd, you are exploiting the bodies of those bystanders as human shields, knowing full well that one of them is more likely to suffer the wrath of the beast than you. If you want to be tough and throw stuff at police, do it the way they did in Tahrir Square: Stand by yourself in the middle of the street. Don't use our bodies as a shield without our permission. Maybe we can organize a time for trigger-happy cops and bottle-throwing "anarchists" to fight without endangering the rest of us. You probably have more in common with each other than you think.

Around midnight, all the black-clad riot police were relieved by new gray units who assumed the front line. They had no badges or patches, no numbers or identifying insignia of any kind, just "SHERIFF" across the front. They had thicker armor and no shields—just batons and zip ties. I figured new units meant new strategy, and decided it was time to leave.

# Riot Cops Don't Like Hugs

During a march through San Francisco in mid-November, around a hundred Occupants deviated from the regular route and took over a Bank of America branch in the Financial District. Bank employees asked them to leave, but instead they pitched a tent in the lobby. That was at 1 PM.

Riot police blocked off the street and filled the bank, while Occupants held their ground. There were ten in the tent, while the rest sat on the floor, or on desks. The whole scene was visible through the large bank windows, where other Occupants from the march gathered.

One by one the police removed the Occupants to wild cheers as they walked them out. Around 6:30 PM, it was time to bust up the tent, but before they did that, they pushed all the Occupants outside, away from the windows. I was pressed right up against the glass, when an officer came and said, "I'm going to have to ask you to back up." Now, thanks to Barry Cooper, I know that "I'm going to have to ask you..." is a phrase cops are trained to use when they want something to sound like an order when it's not. So I asked him, "Is that a request or an order?" His eyes got wide. He wasn't angry, more like bewildered. You'd think no one had ever questioned his authority before. It confused him, but he came around. "Back up, sir. That's an order!" OK, small victory. At least he called me "sir."

I took one step back and allowed him to position himself between me and the window. He kept ordering me to back up, but I only moved as far back as he pushed me with his baton—about ten feet. Once they'd successfully set up their perimeter and the crowd was all away from the window, I tried to strike up a conversation. I asked him how many of the Occupy protests he'd been to. Dead silence. You'd think he didn't even know I was talking to him, but he was staring straight at me. So I asked if he enjoyed making the overtime pay, what he thought of the Occupation, if he liked his job. Stone face.

I asked him if he'd seen the photo of the Occupant in Bogota, Colombia, hugging the riot cop. I had broken through. He didn't say anything. His facial expression didn't change. But he shook his head "no" ever so slightly. So I pushed. "What would you do if I hugged you?" And then he spoke!

"You don't want to do that."

"Yes I do," I replied. "But what would the consequences be?"

He said, "I would arrest you."

"For what?" I persisted.

"Assault."

That's right. This guy who physically pushed me ten feet with a wooden club was prepared to charge me with assault if I hugged him. At that point, the woman next to me chimed in, "Would that be sexual assault or would he have to grab your ass for that?" A look crossed his face that told me instantly he was the type of guy who got uncomfortable whenever anything even vaguely homosexual was mentioned. So I added, "Don't worry. I'd never do anything the TSA wouldn't do."

And then the strangest thing happened. The cop almost, but not quite, smiled.

VICTORY!

It kind of makes sense if you think about it. If you went around hugging people after they asked you not to, it could easily be construed as some kind of sexual assault or sexual harassment. But that's not the point. The point is that I broke through the grayface and got him to give up the silent treatment.

If you ever want to hug a cop... it's a good idea to ask first.

# Dog Fights and Property Rights

Some nights at OccupySF are a comedy of errors. One night the drama unfolded much the way it does in James Joyce's *Ulysses*. No one character in the story was witness to the entire causal chain. But a spectator viewing the actions of many characters may see the thread of unintended consequences.

First some back story. At that time, there was a split occurring within OccupySF, as probably occurred within every Occupation, between democracy and, let's say, "do-ocracy." Those favoring democracy believe in the consensus process of the General Assemblies and those favoring do-ocracy prefer decentralized autonomous direct action. Before a General Assembly, you'll hear someone from the first group walking around yelling, "If you're not at the GA, you're not part of the Movement," and then you'll hear those from the second group laughing at them.

A portion of those in the do-ocracy group constructed something that was loosely being referred to as "the punk house." A lattice of ropes crisscrossed between light posts and palm trees lent support to a shanty structure of tarps and miscellaneous lumber. It was huge, housing at least a dozen Occupants with room enough to even pitch individual tents within the greater structure.

The SFPD issued demands that OccupySF dismantle a considerable portion of the encampment, including the punk house. The police threatened a raid if their demands were not met by that Saturday at noon. So, of course, the demands were discussed at the General Assembly, who essentially agreed to comply. However, the actual Occupants of the punk house weren't at the General Assembly. Conflict ensued. An agreement was negotiated where the punk house could be dismantled if it was replaced by tents that met the demands of the police. Basically they could stay there, but they couldn't attach ropes to the light posts or palm trees. So, two new deluxe tents were purchased from the Occupation's general funds and given to the punks.

Just one problem. When the organizers from the General Assembly arrived with the new tents, the majority of the Occupants of the punk house were not present. After a short shouting match between the organizers and the three or four Occupants who were present, they began dismantling the punk house and piling all the Occupants' personal possessions on the sidewalk. And incidentally, they let out a dog.

The dog, a pit bull, was being kept in the tent while its owner left to get a muzzle. Apparently it had an aggression problem, which the organizers would have known if they had waited for the Occupants before they dismantled the punk house—but then, they only had until noon. In less than an hour, the pit bull attacked another dog in the camp, causing a huge scene, with yelling and punching, as a half dozen Occupants tried to pull the dogs apart.

Then the SFPD arrived. The owner of the dog that was attacked issued a statement and allowed the officer to inspect his animal to see if it needed medical attention, as if some random beat cop has any expertise in veterinary medicine. When the owner of the pit bull arrived back at camp with the muzzle, there was a cop waiting to talk to him.

This incident says so much about unintended consequences, property rights, and self-regulating spontaneous order.

It's interesting to me that the chain begins and ends with police aggression. It's as if the police sent a little spark of aggression into an otherwise peaceful scenario and caused a chain reaction of hostility within the encampment. Then they came in to take a police report on an incident that appears completely unrelated, but that they indirectly caused. In a way, it's similar to an instance of the calculation problem in centrally planned economic systems. The purported purpose of the police demands is public safety, and from the perspective of a central planner, a store-bought pop-up tent is safer than a haphazard amateur construction. But in this specific instance, with this particular tent, leaving the punk house standing, at least until the dog is muzzled, is better for public safety. It's those kind of nuances in individual instances that make central planning completely untenable, and make those closest to the situation the best decision-makers in the vast majority of cases. Also, it's unfortunate that the owner of the dog that was attacked would agree to make a statement to the police. The individual officer may have had the best of intentions, but when a police report of dog-fighting weasels its way through the bureaucracy onto the desks of the decision-makers, it can only hurt the camp. Surely the owner, or even one of the volunteers in the medical tent, were better suited to assess whether or not the dog was injured.

The whole fiasco raises the specter of property rights as well. There is a considerable contingent at OccupySF, especially amongst the do-ocracy and punk house crowd, that doesn't believe in private ownership—but you can sure bet they're upset when their personal possessions are violated by the decisions of the democracy crowd and the General Assembly. The fact is that no liaison should ever have agreed to convey the police demands to the group, because the General Assembly should not have the authority to unilaterally dismantle people's tents or to throw their property into the common area. Fundamentally, this flaw of direct democracy is why many of us have no confidence in the General Assemblies. If police had a problem with the punk house, they should have been told to bring their problem to the individuals involved without threatening the others.

Fundamentally the question that needs to be answered by this incident and incidents like it is: Can spontaneous orders self-regulate or do they require outside aggression to regulate them? If spontaneous orders require outside aggression to regulate them, the General Assembly was right to aggress against the punk house, and the police are right to aggress against the Occupation. But if spontaneous orders do self-regulate, if a dog owner is capable of confining and muzzling an aggressive animal, then we should expect the General Assembly aggressing on the punk house to have unexpected consequences, just as we should expect the police aggressing against the Occupation to have unexpected consequences.

# What the Occupy Movement Could Learn From Somalia

It's time to acknowledge that the Occupy movement is an anarchist movement. *Adbusters*, the magazine that started the ball rolling, describes itself as "anti-consumerist," but it's arguably anarchist, or at least heavily influenced by anarchists.

The hand signals now commonplace at Occupy originated with the Direct Action Network, a confederation of anarchist groups formed to coordinate WTO protests in 1999. And the whole concept of the consensus process used at the General Assemblies comes straight out of anarchist organizing manuals.

Mainstream commentators are baffled, because they are trying to define how this horizontal, leaderless movement intends to influence top-down authoritarian politics. They don't realize that the movement was designed from its outset to replace mainstream politics with a horizontal, leaderless structure, building a new society in the shell of the old, as the saying goes.

There are no demands, because the movement is the demand.

Most of the Occupants probably don't even know this, but it was those familiar with anarchist thought who picked up on these themes and became the early adopters of the movement. Anarchists still represent a minority, but they hold many key organizing positions.

Admittedly, most of them are social anarchists, not market anarchists, but I'm still hoping that the movement expands into a full-blown autonomous anarcho-communist experiment, because nothing spoils someone on communism quite like actually trying it. (Or I could be proven wrong. Either outcome would be excellent.)

I do have one piece of advice. It strikes me as strange that the "social-justice" crowd focuses on legislative processes like democracy, when justice is a judicial process. The movement needs to develop a judicial branch for dispute resolution. I suggest that the Occupy movement look to the existing anarchist judicial method in Somalia, which anthropologist Michael van Notten calls "kritarchy." It could easily be adopted with or without approval from the General Assemblies.

Kritarchy is a judicial process in which justice ("*kritès*" in Greek), rather than written law, is the ruling principle. A kritarchy does not form a court of law. It forms a court of justice, which is completely compatible with the horizontal, leaderless nature of the Occupy movement.

There are two types of justice, commonly symbolized by the

sword and the scales. The sword connotes punitive justice, which assigns punishment for breaking written laws. The scales connote restorative justice, which holds that a person is liable for the damages he causes another person. Kritarchy is only concerned with restorative justice, not punitive justice.

Until someone claims to have suffered an injustice, all behavior is permissible. Disputes are mediated by judges, but it's important to understand that judges do not enjoy any special status. They serve only at the request of the disputants. Anyone in the community may serve as a judge, or request a judiciary be formed, so a court of justice is truly a people's court.

A simple kritarchy involves just three people: two disputants and any third person they approach to help them resolve the injustice. The judge investigates the conflict and attempts to discover the justice between them, to balance the scales. This could be as simple as mediation or as complex as weighing evidence and witness testimony.

The judge decides a case based on the normative customs of the community, and the reason and conscience of the disputants. This judicial model is elegantly suited for the Occupy movement, because it's not based on written law, and it can accommodate a wide diversity of philosophies.

The seeds of a simple kritarchy are already developing in the movement. Normative customs emerge out of people's natural respectful conduct without any written law or central coercive authority; and there are already individuals in the movement developing a reputation for defusing conflicts. They are commonly being called "peacekeepers."

Peacekeepers are already engaged in the first phase of the judicial process in a kritarchy, which van Notten calls "segmental opposition." Whenever there is a physical altercation between two individuals, those around them move in to establish a physical stalemate so that the dispute must be settled with words instead of fists. All that would need to change to make segmental opposition into a simple kritarchy is to transition from having proactive peacekeepers who break up fights to having proactive disputants who seek out peacekeepers to act as judges.

I witnessed a conflict that occurred at OccupySF that could easily have been resolved by a simple kritarchy. Someone left his guitar in the common area while he went to the restroom. While he was gone, another Occupant used it without permission and accidentally broke one of the tuning pegs. This erupted into shouting. Segmental opposition prevented a physical fight, but justice was never satisfied.

A court of justice might have decided that the guitar player was liable for replacing the broken part, or that the guitar owner had been negligent in leaving the guitar in the common area. But either way, the discussion would happen in public, which facilitates the development of normative customs.

Hopefully the disputants honor the decision of the court, but if they refuse, they do so with their own names and reputations on the line.

Enforcement of a verdict requires a more complex kritarchy, and it would likely require the participation of the General Assemblies. Somali society is organized into extended clans, called *xolos*, each composed of many subclans, called *jilibs*. Somali clans are unified by family ties, but they could be replaced by self-selecting groups based on common philosophies or goals. The regional Occupations, for instance, could replace extended clans: Occupy Wall Street, Occupy Denver, Occupy Phoenix, and so on. And the autonomous groups within each occupation could replace subclans.

Clans serve two basic functions for the judicial process. First, judges emerge from the confidence of subclans. So if a dispute occurs between individuals in different subgroups, they may select a judge from each subgroup to decide the case. Second, clans maintain communal funds that members voluntarily contribute to. This fund serves many purposes. Among them, it operates as a social insurance for every member against liability. If a person owes restitution that they cannot or will not pay, the responsibility falls on the subgroup to cover the liability with the communal fund.

This ensures that victims can always be made whole, and also incentivizes clans and subclans to enforce verdicts on their own members, because they are ultimately liable for the damages. The regional occupations already have substantial communal funds of donations that could easily serve this purpose.

A conflict I witnessed at OccupyOakland can help illustrate how a complex kritarchy operates. During one of the marches, the windows of Tully's Coffee were broken. This was particularly egregious because the owner of Tully's Coffee had been a substantial supporter of the Occupation. The café is adjacent to Oscar Grant Plaza, and the owner had allowed activists to use her restrooms and Wi-Fi Internet, and she had made donations of food and money.

The specific Occupants who broke her windows are unknown, because they cover their faces with bandannas, but their subgroup is known and had a regular tent site. In a kritarchy, the owner of Tully's Coffee could serve a claim of injustice against the offending subgroup. A judge representing Tully's Coffee would approach a known judge inside the subgroup and request a Court of Justice be convened, and the two judges would attempt to find agreement over the liability.

If the individuals who broke the windows refused to take responsibility, the damages could be paid by the subgroup collectively. Holding them accountable for their actions would incentivize them to be more judicious with their tactics and membership in the future.

But imagine that an agreement could not be reached. In that case, a third judge would be approached from the extended clan, meaning the General Assembly of OccupyOakland. If this third judge awards damages and neither the individuals nor the subgroup will abide by the verdict, the restitution would come out of the Occupation's general fund.

First and foremost, this prevents the movement from losing the support of its productive members because of the injustices of its destructive members; but also, by placing the burden of injustice on the general fund, you express clearly that the movement will not tolerate injustice internally, and you cause a huge hit to the reputation of those activists who refuse to balance the scales.

If the price of injustice becomes too great, and reputations become too poor, an individual may be cast out of a subgroup, or a subgroup may be cast out of the Occupation to preserve justice. Social ostracism is sufficient to enforce the vast majority of verdicts in Somalia, and it would likely be the only mechanism available to the Occupy movement. (Also, in a kritarchy, an outcast no longer enjoys the protection of any court of justice until they offer restitution.)

Developing a judicial branch of the movement also has exciting and powerful long-term potential. If a simple kritarchy can become a normative custom, and a complex kritarchy can become as firmly established as the General Assemblies are, then we will be able to begin developing a real alternative to the State monopoly of the courts, and the real possibility of Justice will emerge.

# Chapter Ten: Psychoclass A

## The Aftermath

The first light of dawn these days is not white, but amber, when the sun hangs in the penumbra between the horizon and the haze left from the Great Fire.

The morning poured through a broken window, between gimcracks and gadgets, and found the sleeping face of young Hakim. As he stirred, he reached over to his night stand to activate an electric generator.

A few coughs and whirls and the room sprang to life. Lights flashed and flickered, screens ignited and the haunting chords of *Auslander* blasted at full volume. Hakim rolled out of bed into a pile of clothes and emerged in ragged jeans and a "DISOBEY" t-shirt. He walked down an empty hallway past dusty bedrooms to the kitchen, where he boiled water for tea and prepared a simple breakfast of cornmeal porridge, sweet bread, and sesame oil.

It was important to conserve the generator, as petrol was becoming scarce. Hakim generally allowed only an hour for his mobile devices to charge. While he waited, he perused the news of the day. Locally, the weather was clear and the cease-fire had held through the night, which was good for business. Globally, governments continued to collapse in a heap of paper under the weight of their own tedious make-work bureaucracies. The headlines announced that this week Uganda had joined the ranks of the stateless, while the government of New Zealand had followed the precedent led by America and resolved its debt crisis by auctioning off most of its territory to sovereign business franchises, in this case a number of competing pastoral farming and agricultural companies. Hakim was pleased to see that the expected result was a drop in global food prices, but the cost of petrol continued to rise as government subsidies dried up. Yesterday it had spiked 10,000 Kred a barrel.

Hakim was too young to have ever lived under a State. It simply wasn't the custom of the Somali people. To him it was utterly alien to divide society into two classes of rulers and the ruled, and it seemed to him that the only purpose of government was to harass people and eat out their substance.

He finished his breakfast, freshened up, and powered down the generator. No sense leaving it running all day. In his neighborhood, streets were so run down, vehicles couldn't navigate them—not that many people drove anymore. His only neighbors lived in disheveled housing developments defended by private security. Herds of goats grazed grasses that punctuated the concrete guarded by shepherds armed with Kalashnikovs. Vegetable gardens sprang up in any gated lot that had soil. The public rail no longer ran. Public power and water were gone too. Almost all commerce took place near the port, but to get there, he had to walk three full kilometers to reach the private roads.

# New Mogadishu

Once you get within ten kilometers of the port, you have a choice. The local taxi and bus drivers had formed Jidkha Lines, which privately repaired the public roads. Local drivers knew the best routes, and you could negotiate a good price to get anywhere in the city, especially if you don't mind ride-sharing. In addition, Breezeways, a foreign company, had invested in constructing and maintaining a higher quality network of privately owned expressways. The catch was that to gain access to the expressways you had to rent an electric vehicle from their fleet, but those weren't rugged enough for most of the public roads. They were designed for smoother rides.

Hakim had determined that the most cost-effective solution for him was to rent a bicycle from any one of the local shops, because neither company objected to pedestrians and bicyclists using their roads, and it meant his transportation expenses were not subject to the fluctuating price of petrol. In addition, by clipping a drag condenser to the rear wheel, he could generate electricity to charge his mobile devices as he traveled.

Mogadishu had been thrown into chaos by the collapse of the Somali Democratic Republic, torn by decades of civil war. Warlords eager to claim the foreign aid promised by developed nations struggled to establish themselves as the new central government to the exclusion of all others. But as the developed nations began to collapse themselves, the promise of foreign aid disappeared, and with it the incentive for civil war. New Mogadishu had been raised out of the ashes of the old city. Commerce returned, and with it, new prosperity. The lure of completely free trade drew both local entrepreneurs and foreign investors. New Mogadishu quickly became a bustling metropolis, and the telecommunications capital of the world.

Hakim worked as a programmer for Krito Communications. Krito had begun in the US, shielding customers from government attempts to acquire their phone records by every legal means available. They'd then developed numerous encryption algorithms to secure the privacy of their customers' data. But as populist revolutions began springing up around the world, they'd recognized the urgent need for telecommunications that could not be interrupted or intercepted by existing governments. Establishing their headquarters in New Mogadishu had made that possible, and Krito quickly became the world's largest, most impenetrable data haven.

In addition, Krito had launched a private currency called Kred that quickly became the international standard for Internet commerce.

Recognizing the role of hyperinflation in the global economic collapse, Krito had designed the Kred to be entirely digital, which had numerous advantages. First, it could not be manipulated by inflation, because the supply was fixed based on the total number of transactions occurring in the system. Second, it could be transferred using any Krito Communications device, from mobile phones to vehicle GPS systems. The third, and perhaps most innovative advantage, was that Kred represented both "credit" and "credibility." Built into each transaction was an approval rating so that users all have a published reputation evaluation. If users lost their credibility due to dishonest business practices, their Kred was devalued accordingly. The result was an untraceable, decentralized, internationally accepted currency that governments could neither seize nor stop.

# The Pirate Beigh

When Hakim arrived at work, he logged into a half dozen social networking sites. This was actually encouraged by his employer, the idea being that frequent mental micro-breaks leave employees more refreshed and creative than a rigid break schedule does. Internet access was his favorite perk, which he used to manage his more entrepreneurial online activities. This was also encouraged. Krito's policy was that allowing thousands of employees to test their ideas in the market directly was the most fluid laboratory for research and development. The Krito Communications office was a truly modern work environment. Their philosophy was that any free time an employee acquired by completing their regular responsibilities ahead of schedule belonged to them, and that this would not only encourage efficient time management, but everyone would mutually benefit from allowing innovation at all levels of the company.

A message popped onto Hakim's home screen. It was a request from his department head to come to her office. When he walked in, Rose asked him to close the door and have a seat. Whenever this happened, Hakim felt a lurch in the pit of his stomach. There was something about authority itself that made him uneasy. It usually passed as soon as Rose explained the purpose of the meeting.

"I want to talk to you about transferring to a new position in client relations. It would mean a 30,000,000-Kred raise, but there's potentially a whale of a client on the line. It would mean a lot more responsibility."

Rose seemed unusually humble, even conciliatory. Something had spooked her.

"I don't really know that much about client relations. I'm happy to try, but why are you offering this position to me?" Hakim asked.

"The client asked for you by name. But I don't want to say too much. It's better if he tells you himself." She gave him instructions to meet with the client, a man named Beigh, upstairs in the executive lounge.

Hakim ventured into the huge circular room, glancing admiringly at the view from the tall windows overlooking New Mogadishu. People from around the world, speaking dozens of languages, met here to eat and socialize between meetings. Some business travelers actually landed on the rough and never went below the executive lounge. A sense of privacy was still maintained by the sheer vastness of the space. Hakim was clearly out of place, both for his age and his clothes—there was no dress code in the programming office. Even the waitstaff looked more professional than he did.

Across the room a man stood waving to Hakim. Hakim noted that he was unusually tall, like the Mandinka people in West Africa, and dressed all in white, with a dark midnight-black complexion. He extended his hand, with its long round fingers, and shook Hakim's.

"You must be Hakim! I am Beigh. I am very excited to meet you. Please, sit down. Order whatever you like."

Beigh motioned to the menu as Hakim took a seat across from him and began to browse the selections. He'd never eaten anywhere so expensive, or with such diverse cuisine. He wondered if Beigh knew that the custom in New Mogadishu was for the person who extended the invitation to foot the bill. He thought it better not risk it, but even the appetizers were over 20,000 Kred.

Beigh asked, "Do you mind if I conduct a small test of... cognitive ability?" Hakim agreed. "Excellent! Just keep reading the menu. You won't feel a thing."

Beigh popped up and removed some kind of mobile device from his pocket. It looked like a smart phone, or maybe a camera. He held it up to Hakim's head as he walked around the table, and a detailed schematic of the inside of Hakim's brain appeared on the screen.

"Beautiful! Just as I'd hoped," Beigh exclaimed.

"What is it?"

"Your brain. It's marvelous. Not a bruise. Not a hint of scar tissue."

"Scar tissue?" Hakim jumped up, rubbing the back of his head with one hand. "How are you looking in my head?"

Beigh snapped the device closed. "Oh, Hakim. I have so much to share with you! But first I must ask you... do you want to live on a free world?"

"Of course..."

"Good. Let me show you something." Beigh set the device on the table and activated some kind of a projector that suspended a holographic screen above the table. Far more advanced than anything Krito was even close to. The display scrolled through scenes from science fiction movies. A flying saucer demolishing a building with an energy beam. Rows of green men marching in lockstep. A cartoon Martian training his crosshairs on Earth. Laser battles and bug armies, and on and on.

The movie clips scrolled on as Beigh continued. "Do you know what all these stories have in common, Hakim?"

"Aliens?"

"Well, yes. But more than that, they all represent tragic expressions of a primitive psychoclass. They contain depictions of xenophobia, species supremacy, and naked collectivism. On this planet, inter-terrestrial individuals are presumed to be hostile, hive-minded, and fundamentally defined by their planet of birth, rather than by the content of their character. Frankly, it's obscene."

"What's your point? I don't understand what you're getting at."

Beigh laughed softly. "No. I suppose you wouldn't. The point is that I am prepared to deliver hundreds, maybe thousands of foreign merchants, bringing fantastic new technology to this market, but the aggregate of them are only going to feel comfortable trading here if I can demonstrate that a new psychoclass is being born here."

Hakim mulled it over and asked, "Thousands of foreign merchants coming... to Somalia?"

"No, Hakim... coming to Earth."

Hakim jumped back, wide-eyed. "You're an alien! What do you want with me?"

"You are the key, Hakim. The brain scan shows it. I can spot the primitive psychoclass by physical changes in the brain. Scar tissue, really. Adverse childhood experiences cause decreased activity in the prefrontal cortex and a hyperactive amygdala. Tribalism, nationalism, bigotry—these are the symptoms of a damaged brain. A brain incapable of natural empathy. You've probably been told this behavior is normal because every generation of your species until now has shared these traits. But if your brain scan is any indication, something about this has always seemed flawed to you. You are different. I'm sure you've sensed it. You are the proof, maybe the first of your kind, that a generation is coming to this planet that is on the path to *Astaiwah*."

"Where is *Astaiwah*?"

"I forget... it has no equivalent in your language. *Astaiwah* is not a place. It is a direction. It is the future that is approached by the tendency of all sentient life that seeks harmony and autonomy. It is the aggregate of all consensual, mutually beneficial associations."

"What do I have to do?"

"Well... first, you need to see my world."


To Be Continued...

# About Davi

Davi Barker, known online as The Muslim Agorist, is a prolific writer with a passion for philosophy, economics, history and theology. A recipient of the Brass Crescent Award for his investigative style, he advances the Voluntaryist cause with analysis of the confluence of values between Islam and libertarianism as well as contemporary movements from the Tea Party to the Arab Spring. Davi contributes to Examiner.com, The Silver Underground, The Daily Anarchist, Muslims 4 Liberty as well as other publications, and on occasion cooks a mean chicken tikka masala.

All articles in this book originally appeared on one of the following websites:

Examiner.com

IllumeMagazine.com

SilverUnderground.com

DailyAnarchist.com

Muslims4Liberty.org

CPSIA information can be obtained at www.ICGtesting.com
Printed in the USA
LVOW062010150313

324526LV00020B/943/P